Bed & Breakfast
Book

The Scottish Bed & Breakfast Book

Country and Tourist Homes
Farms • Guesthouses • Inns

Second Edition

By June Skinner Sawyers

PELICAN PUBLISHING COMPANY
Gretna 2006

First edition, 2000
Second edition, January 2006

EAN: 9781589802919

Illustrations and maps by Amelia Janes
Front cover photo, Campbell Castle near Inverness, by David Calhoun

Information in this guidebook is based on authoritative data available at the time of printing. Prices listed are subject to change without notice. Readers should take this into account when consulting this guide.

Manufactured in Canada
Published by Pelican Publishing Company, Inc.
1000 Burmaster Street, Gretna, Louisiana 70053

in memory of Bob Prentice,
perfect B&B host and
proud son of Scotland

Contents

Introduction

BACKGROUND

Scotland is one of the most beautiful countries in the world. As anyone who has traveled the many miles within its borders knows, Scotland is also a surprisingly diverse land, ranging from the gently rolling hills of the south to the wild and remote mountainous regions of the north. And yet all is not what it seems, for there are areas of the Lowlands that are much more hilly than what you may find in the Highlands. There's also something about the light and, in the Hebrides, the colors of the sea evoke more Mediterranean blues and greens than the cold waters of the northern isles. But then again Scotland is full of surprises.

At 30,414 square miles, Scotland is a small country—by American standards at least. But size can be deceiving. It's not as easy to get around as one might expect, for example. The roads, although mostly well traveled and relatively easy to navigate once you get the hang of it (which could take several days), nevertheless are smaller and much narrower than North American roads. You'll rarely find a multi-lane motorway in Scotland. On the contrary, the norm in this part of the world are two-lane roads and, in the more remote areas, single-track roads with traffic traveling in both directions (don't worry, passing places are strategically placed every 100 yards or so).

The cultural and historical highlights of Scotland are considerable. Edinburgh not only is the home to the world's largest arts festival, but also hosts one of the liveliest New Year celebrations. Meanwhile, Glasgow, not to be outshined, presents the increasingly popular Celtic Connections festival during the height of winter. (Glaswegians were never ones to allow little things like weather inconvenience them.) Among the newer attractions in Edinburgh surely the most significant must be the Museum of Scotland, which opened in late 1998, and tells the story of Scotland from prehistoric times to the present day. And anyone with even a passing interest in architecture must stop in

Glasgow, the birthplace of Charles Rennie Mackintosh, that misunderstood and under-appreciated genius, as well as stomping grounds for countless unsung architects who plied their trade during the city's grand Victorian age.

Hence, unlike other B&B books, this guide is designed not only to help you find accommodations that best suit your tastes, but also to help you choose areas of the country that appeal to your specific interests. It also helps to know a little bit about a place before venturing into unfamiliar territory. If you want to bone up on your Scottish history and heritage (either in your native soil or while in Scotland itself), you might want to consider the following titles:

• *An Illustrated History of Scotland,* by Elisabeth Fraser (Norwich: Jarrold Publishing, 1997). A readable introduction to Scottish history, this work is profusely illustrated with archival photographs, drawings, and paintings.

• *Highlanders: A History of the Gaels,* by John Macleod (London: Sceptre, London, 1996). This is a compelling history of the Highlands by a popular journalist and fine stylist.

• *Hebridean Odyssey,* edited by Marion Sinclair (Edinburgh: Polygon, 1996). This collection celebrates the unique cultural heritage of the Hebrides in song, prose, poems, and images.

• *Consider the Lilies,* by Iain Crichton Smith (Edinburgh: Canongate, 1995). The Highland Clearances, the Scottish equivalent of the Irish Famine, are presented from the perspective of an old woman evicted from her home.

• *The Scottish Nation: A History 1700-2000,* by T.M. Devine (New York, Viking, 1999). A one-volume general history of modern Scotland.

• *How the Scots Invented the Modern World,* by Arthur Herman (New York: Crown Publishers, 2001). To Herman, being Scottish is more than just a matter of nationality; it is a state of mind. His story then, is how the Scots created the idea of modernity.

The Scottish Tourist Board has about 150 tourist information centers located in towns and villages throughout Scotland. The board also publishes several annual titles, including *Scotland: Bed & Breakfast,* with a listing of over 1,500 establishments (but no detailed descriptions). Other annually updated STB books include *Scotland: Hotels and Guest*

Houses, Scotland: Self-Catering, and *Scotland: Camping & Caravan Parks.*
Information on travel in Scotland can be obtained from the following addresses:

Scottish Tourist Board
19 Cockspur Street
London SW1
Telephone: 0171-930-8661
Scottish Tourist Board Central Information
23 Ravelston Terrace
Edinburgh
(Telephone and written inquiries only)
Telephone: 0131-332-2433
Fax: 0131-315-4545

In the United States
British Tourist Authority
7th floor
551 Fifth Avenue
New York, NY 10176
1-800-GO2-BRITAIN

British Tourist Authority
625 N. Michigan Avenue
Suite 1510
Chicago, IL 60611
Telephone: 1-800-462-2748

In recent years the tourist board has been working diligently to not only aggressively encourage tourism to Scotland but also improve the quality of service, from B&Bs to restaurants and attractions. Thus, any establishment that displays the "Welcome Host" badge indicates that the staff has been trained to provide a higher caliber of service and hospitality. With a few exceptions, I have found this to be true.

The purpose of this book is to present to you descriptions of some of the best B&Bs in Scotland. They were chosen for ambiance, historic appeal, and period charm; sometimes because of their literary connections; and other times based on the warmth and personality of the owners themselves. For make no mistake about it, the B&B owner establishes the mood of the establishment. If they offer enthusiastic and genuine service, you, the guest, will be able to sense their caring attitude straightaway. On the other hand, if they project a suspicious or even hostile mood (and that has sometimes been the case), you'd best stay clear of them altogether.

One time I stayed at what seemed like a perfectly pleasant B&B from the outside, a handsome and charming townhouse that offered splendid views of the cityscape. Unfortunately, the good feeling ended at the front door. The presence of a sterile closed-circuit television screen (to see guests coming and going) and a chilly reception could not compensate for the lovely surroundings. Attitude makes all the difference.

It is important to remember that nothing remains the same. Ownership changes, prices go up, establishments shut down. I have tried to select those establishments that stand out in some (sometimes subtle) ways. You will find descriptions of B&Bs, guesthouses, country inns, small hotels, and farms. With one exception (Nairn's in Glasgow), breakfast is included, which is as it should be. (Nairn's is such an exceptional place that I have chosen to include it anyway.) Write us at the publisher's address with your comments—good or bad. We would love to hear from you about the listings and any new ones that you could recommend for the next edition.

GUARANTEE OF STANDARDS

The Scottish Tourist Board is the official guarantor of quality when it comes to accommodations in Scotland. The new Scottish Tourist Board star system is reportedly the first such system in the world to show the quality level of accommodation by using a star system. The more stars the better the quality. Hence, five stars refers to exceptional or world-class quality, four stars to excellent, three stars to very good, two stars to good, and one star to fair and acceptable.

A trained Scottish Tourist Board inspector grades each property annually. Further information on the star system can be obtained from the British Tourist Authority or at the various tourist information centers throughout Scotland.

A B&B in a private house generally starts from around £20-25 per person, although it can be considerably higher in the cities, especially in places like Edinburgh, depending on the location. Generally speaking, I have chosen to quote either single or double rates (some establishments do not offer single rates at all), based on per-person per-night charges. A B&B usually includes a full Scottish breakfast, and often a snack (biscuits, shortbread, and such) in the evening. (Either way, most rooms have tea- and/or coffee-making facilities). Many B&Bs, especially those in more remote areas, also offer dinner, although at an extra cost. Quite often the dinners at B&Bs are of a higher caliber than those found in local restaurants.

Most hosts will charge an additional few pounds for private facilities.

Given today's competitive climate, where more and more travelers expect higher standards no matter how small the establishment, many B&B owners try to provide *ensuite* accommodations; that is, a room that contains a private bath and/or shower with toilet and sink. Sometimes the host offers a private bath, which can refer to a bath and/or shower that may be located down the hallway or outside your door, but one that is to be used exclusively by you or your traveling companion.

If you are coming to Scotland at the height of the high season—generally June, July, and August—it is best to book in advance. At any time, though, it is highly recommended that you book the first night of your stay no matter what time of the year. You can book before you arrive in several ways: 1) by contacting the individual establishments yourself; 2) through a travel agent; 3) through a major hotel's reservation service; or 4) through the Scottish Tourist Board's Internet site.

When in Scotland you can also book through the tourist information center's local booking service for a minimal fee of around £1, or by using the national Book-A-Bed Ahead service at the various tourist information centers around the country. This service enables you to arrange accommodations for the same evening or several nights in advance in another part of the country. It costs £3 and you must also pay a 10 percent returnable deposit.

All B&Bs listed have either been visited by myself or come highly recommended by friends or professional contacts within the Scottish tourist industry. The B&Bs in the *Scottish Bed & Breakfast Book* are held to our highest standards. Please contact us with your compliments or suggestions, or if you find that any of the lodgings fail to meet your expectations.

PRACTICAL MATTERS

Getting There

There are direct flights to Scotland from several North American destinations, including New York, Chicago (seasonal only), Newark, and Toronto. There are also flights from many European cities, including Amsterdam, Bergen, Brussels, Copenhagen, Dublin, Paris, Reykjavik, and Stavanger. For current information, check with your travel agent or consult the Scottish Tourist Board's latest flight information from your country at www.holiday.scotland.net/os.

In addition, many flight connections can be made within Scotland and to Scotland from other regional airports throughout the United Kingdom.

Money and Changing Currency

By all means do bring traveler's checks. You will feel more comfortable and self-assured for doing so. I would also strongly recommend for both your own benefit and the convenience of the other business party that they be in pounds sterling.

Banks are usually open Monday to Friday, between 9 A.M. to 4 or 5 P.M. Some banks are open late on Thursdays and a few are even open on Saturday mornings. Scottish banks issue their own bank notes that are legal tender in England as well (no matter what the English say). Banks usually offer the best exchange rates. Of course it is also possible to change money in airports, at some of the larger railway stations, with travel agents, and at the larger hotels (but only if you are a resident). There is usually a small handling fee and commission involved.

Credit cards are widely accepted throughout Scotland, although smaller accommodations or accommodations in more remote areas may not accept them. I have found that VISA is more widely accepted than MasterCard or American Express. Even so, it is always advisable to carry at least some cash or pound sterling traveler's checks around with you.

TRANSPORTATION

Rental Cars

It is usually cheaper to rent your car before arriving in Scotland. Check with your local travel agent.

Major international rental car companies are all represented in Scotland; again it is best to book through your travel agent. Most companies require the driver to be between 23 and 70, while having held a current driving license for at least one year. Note: If you prefer an automatic transmission, it is imperative that you reserve in advance.

A word of advice about driving in Scotland's four major cities (Glasgow, Edinburgh, Aberdeen, and Dundee): Don't.

Another word of advice on driving in Scotland: Stay left. Scotland, like the rest of the United Kingdom, drives on the left side of the road. It's an easy thing to forget, especially in the heat of the moment or when you're ogling a particularly beautiful sight. Just to be on the safe side a friend of mine always plants a large handwritten "KEEP LEFT" sign on the dashboard of the driver's side. It serves as an unobtrusive mental reminder.

Any holder of an overseas driving license may for a period of up to one year drive a car in Britain. The speed on dual carriageways (two-lane roads) is 70 mph, on single carriageways 60 mph, and residential areas 30 mph, unless otherwise signposted. Throughout Britain, it is compulsory for all car occupants to wear seat belts, unless the rear seats are not so equipped.

Motorist's tip: Watch out for the white-on-brown with a blue thistle road signs showing National Tourist Routes and visitor attractions. There are 12 of these routes, which take you along quieter roads and through the countryside. They usually traverse some of the country's most spectacular scenery.

Buses

Scotland has an extensive bus network. Indeed, buses travel to the smallest of towns. Scottish Citylink, in particular, serves all major cities and towns in Scotland, as well as some of the more outlying locations. National Express operates several times daily from London to Edinburgh and Glasgow.

Numerous companies operate bus services to or in Scotland, such as Skye-ways Express or Highland Country Buses. Advanced reservations are not usually required. The following are some useful numbers:

To and within Scotland
Scottish Citylink Coaches
990-505050

National Express
990-808080

Remote communities often use the more than 140 local services of the Royal Mail Postbuses, which not only deliver mail but also transport passengers, when there is no other form of public transport, for a nominal fee. For schedules contact Tel.: 0131-228-7407.

Trains

Although train travel in Scotland (and throughout the rest of Britain, for that matter) is not what it used to be, with so much privatization going on, it is still infinitely better than the service on this side of the ocean. The wise and economically frugal traveler will take full advantage of it.

Scotland's rail service provides excellent InterCity services between all major U.K. cities, as well as good internal links. The journey from London to Edinburgh, for example, takes about four hours, and about five hours from London to Glasgow. GNER, Virgin, and ScotRail operate rail services to points within Scotland. ScotRail publishes a monthly complimentary magazine, *Horizons,* which is available on most of the major lines.

For more information contact National Rail Enquiries by telephone at 08457-484950, consult their web site at www.scotrail.co.uk, www.gner.co.uk, or nationalrail.co.uk, or contact British Rail international branches:

Canada
Rail Europe
2087 Dundas Street East, #105
Mississauga, Ontario L4X 1M2

United States
BritRail
1500 Broadway, 10th floor
New York, NY 10036
Telephone: 212-382-3737
Fax: 212-575-2542

Ferries

Scotland has almost 800 islands, of which some 130 are inhabited. Caledonian MacBrayne (Tel.: 990-650000) offers services to 23 islands and 54 ports off the west coast and in the Firth of Clyde; most carry vehicles and passengers. The summer schedule operates from Easter to mid-October, although there is reduced service the rest of the year.

Other ferry services include Western Ferries (0141-332-9766), P&O Scottish Ferries (1224-572615), John o'Groats Ferries (1955-611353), Orkney Ferries (1856-872044), and Shetland Islands Council ferries (1806-244234).

Weather

People don't usually come to Scotland for the weather. They come in spite of it. That's just a way of saying that Scottish weather is unpredictable.

May and June are usually the driest months. The east coast tends to be cool and dry, the west milder and wetter. But these are only general guidelines, and within minutes upon your arrival in Scotland may be proven resolutely wrong. The average daily temperature during the summer months is 15-22 degrees centigrade.

Best piece of advice: layer. No matter how warm it may be during the day, always have another layer of clothing handy. You never know when the weather is going to change. Although it may be a bit bulky, you'll appreciate the extra warmth and comfort of the layers when the wind changes direction and the temperatures dip precipitously. And during those lucky instances when you are absolutely roasting, simply shed, shed, and shed again (within reason, of course).

BOOKING AHEAD

Booking Outside Scotland

It is always wise to book ahead, especially during high season. And even if departing during the shoulder season (May or September), it's still a good idea to book at least for the first night. That way you'll feel more secure knowing that when you land the next morning—all bleary-eyed and ready for a real bed—you'll at least know you have a place to rest your weary body.

If calling from the United States dial 1, then 011 (the international code), then 44 (the country code), and then the phone number itself. Typically no advance payment or credit card is required to hold a room.

Booking Inside Scotland

Booking ahead in Scotland is even easier. You simply phone the hosts and tell them approximately what time you will be arriving. In addition, many hosts would be more than happy to book ahead for you at no extra charge if you ask.

GENERAL INFORMATION ABOUT LODGINGS

Rooms

Generally speaking, the bedrooms in Scotland are smaller than what most North Americans are probably accustomed to. I have tried to choose accommodations that have character or are in some way unique. Ambiance goes far in this book.

Meals

Upon arrival, many hosts will offer you tea. Now mind you, "tea" is not merely a cup of the ubiquitous liquid, but rather a full repast all its own: it could include scones, tea breads, biscuits, shortbread, or other homemade goodies. (In Scotland you don't need to go to bed on an empty stomach if you don't want to.) When you arrive, do remind the host of any special or vegetarian dietary requests. If you arrive earlier in the day, you may discuss dinner plans with your host.

A full Scottish breakfast typically consists of eggs cooked to order, bacon, sausage, tomatoes (usually the stewed variety), toast or bread with butter or jam, juice, and cereal (muesli is on most menus; porridge is less common nowadays). Yogurt and fresh fruit or fruit compotes are increasingly showing up on breakfast menus. And don't be too surprised to find salmon, kippers, and occasionally haggis on your breakfast plate too.

Booking Tours and Events

Your host will be more than happy to book any tours or shows in the area. I have found that most B&B owners try to keep up with what's happening in their immediate vicinity. At the very least, they usually have brochures describing upcoming attractions.

Telephoning in Scotland

Inside Scotland you can phone with coins or with a phone card. Phone cards can be bought at post offices, news agents, and tourist information centers. Since hotels charge such high rates, you're better off using public telephones. Some of the B&Bs have coin box telephones where you can make local calls for 20 pence or so (keep your coins handy just in case).

When phoning from outside Scotland, dial your country's international access code (011 in the United States; xx in Canada) followed by 44. Then dial the area code minus the first 0 and then the phone number.

Scotland on the Web

For those who prefer to obtain their information quickly and with little effort, there are several Web sites that may be of use:

British Tourist Authority Web site:
www.visitbritain.com
www.holiday.scotland.net/os

Edinburgh and Scotland Information Centre Web site:
www.edinburgh.org

Glasgow Tourist Information Centre e-mail:
TourismGlasgow@ggcvtb.org.uk

The official website of Scotland's National Tourism Board is www.visitscotland.com.

Laundry

Because of their size, most B&Bs do not have laundry service—at least officially. Having said that, there have been numerous times when a B&B owner, perhaps taking pity on my limited wardrobe supply, offered to do my laundry free of charge. Although not a common occurrence, it can—and does—happen.

Handicapped Facilities

Although it still leaves a lot to be desired, Scotland offers a wide range of facilities suitable for people with disabilities. These include visitor attractions, accommodations, and shops. The Scottish Tourist Board produces an information guide designed to assist visitors with disabilities to find appropriate sources. For further information contact:

Disability Scotland
Princes House
5 Shandwick Place
Edinburgh EH2 4RG
Telephone: 0131-229-8632
Fax: 0131-229-5168

Smoking

In recent years smoking in public places has noticeably decreased in Scotland, from restaurants and accommodations and even in pubs. In fact, more and more places, including bed and breakfasts, are banning smoking altogether. This trend will only continue. In November 2004, the Scottish Parliament announced a ban on smoking in public places in Scotland. It is to be fully implemented by Spring 2006.

Security

Scotland is generally a safe country. But, as with most countries today, crime is on the upswing, especially in urban areas. It's best to lock your car at all times, and by all means keep your valuables in the trunk or simply out of plain sight. Although as a woman traveling alone I have never experienced any trouble, it is best to always keep your wits about you, especially at night or in unfamiliar areas.

The Scottish Bed & Breakfast Book

BORDERS

The Borders

The Borders is best described as the land that got away. It is one of the more subtly beautiful parts of Scotland, and also an area that exudes an aura of tranquility, which is ironic given the area's violent past.

The name that is intricately associated with the Borders is Sir Walter Scott. Abbotsford House, his expansive estate and now a fine museum, is located just three miles west of the town of Melrose. Any visit to Abbotsford will showcase his study, library (with its more than 9,000 volumes shelved away), drawing room, armoires, and dining room overlooking the Tweed. It was here that he died in September 1832.

The Borders covers an area of approximately 1,800 square miles. It is a surprisingly diverse landscape that ranges from gently rolling hills to rocky coasts. The Borders also contains one of the longest rivers in Britain, the Tweed, which runs for about 100 miles through the area and at one point forms the natural border between Scotland and England.

For more than 300 years, from the late fourteenth century to the Union of Crowns in 1603, the Borders witnessed an endless succession of feuds and thievery, violence and turmoil. Blood flowed all too often through its streams and rivers. Perhaps it is because of this deep-rooted anguish that the Borders offers one of the richest folk cultures in the country. The ordinary men and women of the area created their own musical genre—that of the Border ballads, wild and wildly entertaining stories populated by a larger-than-life cast of characters and fraught with the very real prospect of danger.

More than most areas of Scotland, Border towns seem especially keen on promoting a very high level of community involvement. This is most visibly expressed in the fervor associated with the local sport, rugby, but also in the Common Ridings that take place throughout the summer months, when everybody seems to get involved. These annual events commemorate a time when community boundaries required protection from outsiders. In late March the town of Hawick celebrates the annual Reivers Festival (reivers were cattle thieves and outlaws).

Elsewhere in the Borders you will find excellent woolen mills and shops, as well as the romance of the great, and ruined, Border abbeys, particularly Melrose, Jedburgh, Kelso, and Dryburgh. Scott is buried here amid the abbey ruins. What a suitably romantic site indeed for this most romantic of Scottish figures! The Border towns of Selkirk, Peebles, and Hawick are also worth visiting.

One of the moodiest of castles is Hermitage Castle, which sits in splendid isolation along a remote tract of road in a lonely glen. It's not easy to get to, but what a sight to behold when you eventually arrive: a marvelous relic of a castle, squat and foreboding and full of deep, dark secrets. Mary, Queen of Scots, spent several hours here in 1566, and they're still talking about it.

Burts Hotel
Graham, Anne, and Nicholas Henderson
Market Square
Melrose
Telephone: 01896-822285
Fax: 01896-822870
E-mail: burtshotel@aol.com
Web site: www.burtshotel.co.uk
Bedrooms: 20, all ensuite.
Rates: £50 pp. **Credit cards:** MasterCard/Eurocard, American Express, VISA, Switch, Delta, JCB. **Open:** All year except December 24-27. **Children:** Yes. **Pets:** Dogs only. **Smoking:** No smoking in bedrooms and restaurant; smoking in bar and bistro only. **Provision for handicapped:** Yes. **Directions:** On the A6091, 2 miles from A68, 38 miles south of Edinburgh. Located in the town square.

This restored family-run eighteenth-century hotel is ably and cheerfully operated by the Henderson family: Graham, Anne, and Nicholas. Set in the town's market square, Burts has been a local landmark for generations—it was built in 1722 as a comfortable home for a prominent local. Although the historic building has been thoroughly modernized, it still retains its period charm. For more than 35 years it has been personally overseen by Graham and Anne. Over the years they have been joined in the family business by their son, Nicholas, and his wife, Trish. Each room is individually decorated. Sitting for a few moments by the glowing fireplace or having a drink in the lounge bar is a pleasant way to start the evening. The bar has over 60 malt whiskies. You are also welcome to enjoy the private hotel garden.

There's a comfortable resident's lounge on the first floor, and a Taste of Scotland restaurant on the premises that specializes in local game, fish, and poultry, seasonal salads, veggies, and fruits. Fare specific to the Borders might include wedges of Teviotdale cheese with smoked salmon, served with a whiskey marmalade, followed by a Border lamb rolled with wild mushrooms and spinach and accompanied by minted apple chutney. For dessert, try the Selkirk bannock pudding with lemon and shortbread ice cream. The Borders has 19 golf courses. Melrose's golf club is located in an elevated position, with views over Scott country.

Dunfermline House Guest House
Bryan and Alison Bell
3 Buccleuch Street
Melrose
Telephone: 01896-822411
E-mail: dunfermline.house@virgin.net
Web site: www.dunfermlinehouse.co.uk
Bedrooms: 5; 4 ensuite, 1 single with private bathroom.
Rates: £25. **Credit cards:** No. **Open:** All year. **Children:** Yes. **Pets:** No.
Smoking: No. **Provision for handicapped:** No. **Directions:** From
Melrose follow directions for Melrose Abbey. Dunfermline House is
opposite the Abbey car park.

New owners Bryan and Alison Bell run a handsome Victorian townhouse that is located in a former town saddlery. It is now one of the
longest established and most respected guesthouses in the area and,
best of all, conveniently located about 50 yards from famous Melrose
Abbey. The abbey, a warm reddish sandstone ruin, has a terrific history
of its own to tell. Founded in 1136 by Cistercian monks at the behest
of King David I, Melrose soon became one of the wealthiest monas-
teries in Scotland and held one of the largest sheep farms in Europe.
Time and raiding took its toll over the centuries. What you see today is
mostly from the fifteenth and sixteenth centuries. After poking
around the romantic ruins or sightseeing around the surrounding
countryside, the Grahams offer a cozy place to return to. Don't forget to try their traditionally made porridge and homemade jams and
marmalades in their comfortable dining room.

Tibbie Shiels Inn
Mrs. J. Brown
St. Mary's Loch
Selkirkshire
Telephone: 01750-42231
Bedrooms: 5 rooms; 1 with bath, 4 with showers.
Rates: £24 single. **Credit cards:** VISA, Delta, MasterCard. **Open:** Closed Monday, Tuesday, and Wednesday from November to Easter. **Children:** Yes. **Pets:** No. **Smoking:** Yes. **Provision for handicapped:** Yes. **Directions:** Situated between St. Mary's Loch and the Loch of the Lowes on the A708 Selkirk to Moffat Road.

Tibbie Shiels must surely be one of the most famous historical inns in Scotland. Established in 1826, this whitewashed lodging has strong associations with Sir Walter Scott, William Wordsworth, and James Hogg. Indeed, a statue of a seated Mr. Hogg stands across the busy road.

Situated on the isthmus between St. Mary's Loch and the Loch of the Lowes, it takes its name from Isabella (Tibbie) Shiel, who moved with her husband, Robert Richardson, a mole catcher, in 1823 into what was then known as St. Mary's Cottage, on the estate of Lord Napier. After the death of her husband the following year, the irrepressible Tibbie determined to support herself and her six children by taking in "gentlemen lodgers." Tibbie apparently had a great sense of humor, and there are countless stories that attest to that. She died in 1878 in her 96th year, but until then she forever played the charming hostess.

Publisher Robert Chambers was an early visitor, while another regular was the aforementioned Mr. Hogg, the writer and poet (best known today for his psychological novel *The Private Memoirs and Confessions of a Justified Sinner)*. It seems that Tibbie was an old friend of Hogg—she had worked as a girl in his mother's household—and was totally unimpressed by his writing. Other prominent visitors included Robert Louis Stevenson, Thomas Carlyle, and Prime Minister William Gladstone. It's still a popular stop, especially for those walking the Southern Upland Way. Sailing and windsurfing are available on the loch. As to be expected in such a venerable place, the low-ceilinged inn is cozy and full of great character. Afternoon tea is available from £3.75, high tea from £8, and dinner from £5-11.50. Free fishing is available for guests.

Gordon Arms Hotel
John McCann
Yarrow Valley
By Selkirk
Telephone: 01750-82222
Bedrooms: 6 rooms.
Rates: £26 pp. **Credit cards:** No. **Open:** Year-round. **Children:** No. **Pets:** No. **Smoking:** Yes. **Provision for handicapped:** No. **Directions:** Between Selkirk and Moffat on the A708 Road.

This family-run and historic hotel lies along the A708 just west of Selkirk. Literary fans should especially find it significant, for here reportedly took place the last meeting between Sir Walter Scott and James Hogg. Scott is of course the great Scots novelist and Hogg an important writer and poet in his own right. From a Borders perspective, what makes it even more fascinating is that both figures were prominent ballad collectors as well. And the area around the Gordon Arms has rich associations with the great Border ballad tradition. Indeed, one of the most poignant and heartbreakingly sad of the ballads, "The Dowie Dens o' Yarrow," is set in this area. The current owner, John McCann, is an ex-firefighter, so one suspects that he has quite a few tales of his own to share with his guests. Good home cooking is offered at the Gordon Arms, while homemade bread is a specialty. Real ales and single malt whiskies are on tap. Hillwalking, cycling, and fishing are just some of the outdoor activities available in the immediate area.

ALSO RECOMMENDED

Duns, *St. Albans,* Mrs. Hannay, Clouds Lane. Telephone: 01361-883285. Fax: 01361-884534. 1 room, with private facilities. Attractive Georgian house with tranquil and secluded garden. Offers magnificent views over the Cheviot Hills. Quiet location. Non-smoking.

By **Eyemouth,** *Redhall Cottages,* Joan Binns, Ayton. Telephone: 018907-81488. 3 rooms, all ensuite. Utterly charming cottages in a very quiet setting. Golf packages are available. No children. Non-smoking.

Innerleithen, *Caddon View Guest House,* 14 Pirn Road. Telephone: 01896-830208. 6 rooms; 5 ensuite and 1 private. Victorian-era home known for its French home cooking. Free use of sauna.

Innerleithen, *St. Ronans Hotel,* Peeblesshire. Telephone: 01896-831487. 6 rooms. Family-owned and operated 1820s historic inn. Past guests have included none other than Sir Walter Scott and Robert Burns. Handsome textured white brick exterior.

Kelso, *Bellevue House,* Jo Bradley, Bowmont Street. Telephone/Fax: 01573-224588. 6 rooms, all ensuite. Charming building built in the 1860s and once home to the angler and poet Thomas Stoddart. Non-smoking. Near town center, Floors Castle, and the River Tweed.

Melrose, *Little Fordel,* Louise Buchanan, Abbey Street. Telephone: 01896-822206. 2 rooms, both ensuite. Pretty B&B housed in a former schoolhouse and located in a quiet cul-de-sac in the center of town.

Melrose, *The Townhouse Hotel,* Market Square. Telephone: 01896-822645. Fax: 01896-823474. 11 rooms, all ensuite. Small, cheery hotel with modern conveniences. Located in the heart of town.

Peebles, *The Horse Shoe Inn,* Mr. and Mrs. Hathaway, Eddleston. Telephone: 01721-730225. Fax: 01721-730268. E-mail: Derek.hathaway@virgin.net. Web site: www.horseshoeinn.com. 8 rooms. Small, charming country inn on the outskirts of Peebles.

Peebles, *Lindores,* Mr. and Mrs. C. Lane, Old Town. Telephone/Fax: 01721-720441. E-mail: lane.lindores@virgin.net. 4 rooms, 2 ensuite. Excellent food is served by an award-winning chef in this spacious and attractive house.

By **Peebles,** *The Shieling,* John and Joan Richardson, Eshiels. Telephone/Fax: 01721-722577. 3 rooms, 1 ensuite. Modern country house located in half-acre garden. Offers lovely views over the Tweed Valley. Located about .5 mile from Peebles.

St. Boswells, *The Clachan,* Nina Johnstone, Main Street. Telephone: 01835-822266. 3 rooms. Large, comfy home located on the edge of the village of St. Boswells. Boasts a log fire. Close to the River Tweed, fishing, and golf. Evening meals served. Walkers please note: this is a perfect location for walking St. Cuthbert's Way, a 2.5-mile pilgrimage route that stretches from Melrose to Lindisfarne in England.

St. Boswells, *Greenside Farm,* Moira Steel, by Melrose. Telephone: 01835-822140. 6 rooms, all ensuite. Victorian farmhouse located in the center of the small village of St. Boswells.

DUMFRIES & GALLOWAY

N

to Edinburgh

A7

Gilnockie Tower
Canonbie
Kirkpatrick Fleming
Gretna Green
Gretna

A7

Langholm

Eskdalemuir

Lockerbie

Ecclefechan

M6

Annan

A75

Ruthwell

Moffat

Devil's Beef Tub
A701
Beattock

A74
M6

A709

Lochmaben

A701

Kirkbean
Carsethorn

New Abbey

Kirkpatrick Durham

Dalbeattie

Kippford

Dumfries and Galloway

A591

A596

A595

A594

A590

Solway Firth

A66

to Glasgow

M74

A74

Wanlockhead

Kirkconnel

Sanquhar

River Nith

A76

NITHSDALE

Dumfries

A75

A712

A711

Castle Douglas

A74

A711

Auchencairn

Dundrennan

Moniaive

A702

St. John's Town of Dalry

Balmaclellan

New Galloway

Parton

Loch Ken

A713

A762

Clatteringshaws Loch

Galloway Forest Park

A712

A755

Gatehouse of Fleet

Kirkcudbright

Creetown

Wigtown Bay

A713

A77

A719

A714

Newton Stewart

A75

A714

Wigtown

Bladnoch

A746

Chapel Finian

The Machars

Port William

Whithorn

Isle of Whithorn

Cairnryan

Stranraer

Castle Kennedy

Glenluce

A747

Luce Bay

Mull of Galloway

Corsewall Point

Loch Ryan

A77

A718

The Rhinns of Galloway

Portpatrick

A716

Firth of Clyde

0   10 miles
0   10 kilometers

Dumfries & Galloway

Dumfries and Galloway has everything that many visitors to Scotland would desire—sparkling lochs, moody peaks, rolling hills, smart and attractive towns, and enough outdoor activities to keep even the most active traveler busy for days on end.

Yet this area remains one of Scotland's most neglected corners. Perhaps the reason for the neglect is its location, a relatively remote section in the southwestern corner of the country, or perhaps it has more to do with its low profile. Whatever the reason, it is a shame, for Dumfries and Galloway has a lot to offer.

The commercial center of the region is Dumfries, an attractive big town that has rich associations with Robert Burns, Scotland's national bard (the Burns Statue is located smack in the center of town). Burns spent his last years here. He and his family lived at the house on Burns Street, now called the Burns House, until his death in 1796. Burns also spent many an enjoyable hour at the famous Globe Inn, off High Street. This is truly a wonderful place—with or without Burns. It boasts great atmosphere, friendly service, and terrific food. An inn since 1610, it contains much of interest to Burns enthusiasts and non-enthusiasts alike: his favorite chair, bowl, and ladle, and if you ask a staff member they will take you upstairs to see where the poet etched a few stanzas in the bedroom window.

Dumfries and Galloway contains several pretty small towns and villages. During the eighteenth and early nineteenth centuries, Gatehouse of Fleet was a solid cotton manufacturing town. James Murray, the local laird, planned the building of the town and the erection of the mills. The Bobbin Mill, the last remnant in Gatehouse of the Industrial Revolution, closed as recently as the 1930s and has since been converted into an award-winning museum. It is certainly worth a visit.

However, no town in the district is as charming as Kirkcudbright, strategically and handsomely located on a harbor. Take the time to leisurely walk down its narrow streets. Palm trees, attractive old houses, and a mild climate drew many artists here, as early as the 1880s. But its art colony credentials really came to complete fruition in the late 1920s, when artists such as E.A. Hornel, Jessie M. King, and S.J. Peploe, among others, either settled or summered here. The work of contemporary artists is on display at places like the Harbour Cottage Gallery and the Tolbooth Arts Centre.

Historic figures also left their mark in Dumfries and Galloway. Thomas Carlyle, the crusty man of letters who later moved to London and became known as the "Sage of Chelsea," was born in the town of Ecclefechan. His house is located here, off the A74, where you can view his collection of photographs, manuscripts, letters, and other related paraphernalia.

It's hard to believe that the origins of the American navy lie in this part of the world. Yet it was here in Kirkbean, in a corner of Scotland known as the Garden of Galloway, that John Paul Jones was born in a small, whitewashed, two-room cottage. There is a museum and audio-visual program that relates the young naval hero's victories during the Revolutionary War. It also includes a recreation of the cabin aboard his ship, the *Bonhomme Richard*.

Moffat boasts of having the widest main street in Scotland. This former sheep and wool trading center is best symbolized by the bronze statue of the Moffat Ram that stands proudly on High Street. Woolen shops as well as ice cream and toffee shops line the broad thoroughfare.

Much of what you see today dates from the nineteenth century, when Moffat was known as a Victorian spa town and flocks of people came here, by railway in those days, to savor its soothing mineral waters. The local Moffat Museum, housed in a former bakery, tells the story of Moffat, including its days as a popular spa center.

Moffat is fortunate to be near several natural landmarks that are worth seeking out. The Grey Mare's Tail on the A708 refers to a spectacular 200-foot waterfall, while the Devil's Beeftub on the A701 is a natural depression used by reivers, or thieves, for hiding stolen cattle in the bad old days.

Another town worth visiting is Whithorn, a market center that is surrounded by many fascinating archeological sites and monuments. Most fascinating of all is the cult of St. Ninian, Scotland's first saint, which flourished in the area for more than a thousand years. Ninian is said to have built his small stone church, the Candida Casa, or White House, here, said to be the first Christian church in Scotland. The Whithorn Priory and Museum along the main street contains the ruins of a twelfth-century priory. Whithorn was also a popular place of pilgrimage, especially for Scottish monarchs. While here, do take the time to visit the Whithorn Discovery Centre, which tells the story of Scotland's first Christian settlement—archeologists have been excavating the site since 1986. Their discoveries are also on display at the center.

The town of Newton Stewart is a good base for forays into Galloway Forest Park, which is studded with lochs, woods, and hills. If you really want to go off the beaten track, though, then hightail it to the Rhinns of Galloway, the peninsula that juts out into the Irish Sea. The southern portion of the peninsula will eventually take you to the Mull of Galloway, with its splendid views of Ireland, the Isle of Man, Cumbria in England, and the Galloway Hills.

Murray Arms Hotel
Ann Street
Gatehouse-of-Fleet
Telephone: 01557-814207
Fax: 01557-814370
E-mail: murrayarmshotel@ukonline.co.uk
Web site: www.murrayarms.com
Bedrooms: 13 rooms, all ensuite.
Rates: £55 single pp. - £95 twin/double pp. **Credit cards:** American Express, MasterCard, Diners Club, VISA. **Open:** All year. **Pets:** Yes. **Smoking:** Restricted. **Provision for handicapped:** No. **Directions:** Off the A75, midway between Dumfries and Stranraer. The hotel is located by the clock tower.

Established over 300 years ago, this old coach inn was also patronized by Robert Burns. Indeed, the peripatetic poet wrote "Scots Wha Hae," one of his most famous songs and Scotland's unofficial national anthem, here. Ask to see the Burns Room, where he actually wrote the poem. The hotel has 13 comfortable rooms, 3 public rooms (bars), and the Lunky Hole Restaurant, which makes good use of Galloway's fine produce. In addition to Burns, generations of Scots and visitors alike have spent many a pleasant night at the Murray Arms. Except for a brief time, for most of its history the Murray Arms has been part of the Cally Estate. James Murray of Broughton and Cally built the inn in 1760. The portion of the building that is now used as the coffee room existed prior to 1642, and was at one time the only house in town (referred to as the Gait House of the River Fleet and thus the town's current name). The keeper of the gait, or road to the ford across the River Fleet, lived here. Within walking distance from the inn are many historical buildings, including the Mill on the Fleet, which served as the center of the town's once-flourishing cotton industry.

Baytree House
Jackie Callander
110 High Street
Kirkcudbright
Telephone/Fax: 0870-835-8448
Web site: www.baytreehouse.net
Bedrooms: 3 rooms, all ensuite.
Rates: From £30 pp. **Credit cards:** None. **Open:** All year. **Children:** All ages. **Pets:** Small pets. **Smoking:** No. **Provision for handicapped:** Two ground floor bedrooms are large enough for wheelchairs. **Directions:** Travel along the main A75 route going west. Take the 711 road to Kirkcudbright. Drive straight through town until you come to High Street. Baytree is located halfway along the road, at the junction of High and Castle Streets.

Located near the harbor in the old quarter of this pretty artist's colony, Baytree is an old Georgian townhouse with the original woodwork and fireplaces still intact. Its impressive drawing room comes complete with vaulted ceiling and ornate cornices. There is also a huge drawing room on the first floor, with an open fire. Jackie moved to the area in 1995, thoroughly renovated the house, and opened for business in February 1997.

There is a garden (about .75 acres altogether), considered one of the finest in Kirkcudbright, which contains a small pond surrounded by old stone walls. One of the Baytree's double rooms has a fourposter bed and Victorian bath. The garden room is a self-contained unit, with its own kitchen, bathroom, bed, and even its own conservatory (glass-covered area), where you can have breakfast served. Hence, those who stay in the garden room can come and go as they please. Each room retains its own personality though, and is tastefully decorated. In warm weather, you can sit and relax on the sundeck. The B&B also contains a fine collection of antiques and paintings, the latter by Kirkcudbright artists. All the food is homemade. A typical breakfast may consist of scrambled eggs made with cream and served with smoked salmon and fennel. A traditional clootie dumpling (a pudding typically made with butter, syrup, treacle, egg, milk, and flour) comes accompanied with a traditional Scottish breakfast. Dinner is a treat, too. Jackie uses all local game and fish (salmon, scallops, trout, etc.) as well as fresh raspberries and strawberries from the garden. Afternoon teas are also offered. Kirkcudbright is known for its mild climate. It even boasts palm trees.

Selkirk Arms Hotel
John and Sheila Shearer
High Street
Kirkcudbright
Telephone: 01557-330402
Fax: 01557-331639
E-mail:
reception@selkirkarmshotel.co.uk
Web site: www.selkirkarmshotel.co.uk
Bedrooms: 16 rooms, all ensuite.
Rates: £67.50 single pp. - £97.50 double pp. **Credit cards:** MasterCard/
Eurocard, American Express, VISA, Diners Club, Switch, Delta, JCB.
Open: All year except Christmas Day. **Children:** Yes. **Pets:** Yes. **Provision
for handicapped:** Restricted. **Directions:** Located on the east end of
Kirkcudbright's High Street.

The Selkirk Arms, located on a quiet residential street, is probably
the best-known hotel in Kirkcudbright, and certainly one of the oldest.
Dating back to 1770, this historic hotel has witnessed many changes in
the area and played host to many visitors (Robert Burns stayed here in
1794, and it was here that he wrote "The Selkirk Grace"). Today's owners, John and Sheila Shearer, continue in that grand tradition. The
modernized version of the Selkirk Arms serves several functions.

On the one hand it is most certainly a handsome hostelry, provid-
ing all the amenities that the contemporary traveler expects and,
indeed, demands. But it also houses a fine gourmet restaurant, where
the service is professional and the staff friendly without being over-
bearing. The restaurant overlooks a large and secluded garden. The
coat of arms on the hotel sign belongs to Thomas Douglas, the Earl
of Selkirk, a Kirkcudbright native and the man responsible for the
founding of what would become the modern Canadian city of
Winnipeg. A short walk away from the hotel, the Broughton House
and Gardens is a handsome Georgian mansion and the former home
of E. A. Hornel, considered the founder of Kirkcudbright's artist's
colony. The museum contains many of Hornel's paintings and a
Japanese-style garden in the back.

ALSO RECOMMENDED

Ecclefechan, *Cressfield Country House Hotel,* Mr. and Mrs. Arthur, Townfoot, Dumfries-shire. Telephone: 01576-300281. Fax: 01576-204218. 10 rooms, all ensuite. This handsome sandstone building was constructed in the nineteenth century and was designed by Thomas Carlyle's father.

Gatehouse-of-Fleet, *The Bay House,* Carole Jackson, 9 Ann Street. Telephone: 01557-814073. 3 rooms, 2 ensuite. A lovely B&B, small and cozy, overlooking garden, with a riot of flowers overflowing from windowsills. Peaceful setting any way you look at it.

Gatehouse-of-Fleet, *The Cree Gallery,* Linda Hepburn, 56 High Street. Telephone/Fax: 01557-814458. 2 rooms; 1 double and 1 family. Comfortable accommodation situated above an art gallery and antique shop. The work of contemporary artists from England and Scotland is on display. And in an unusual twist, breakfast is served in the gallery.

Kirkbean, *Cavens House Hotel,* Kirkbean, by Dumfries. Telephone/Fax: 01387-880234. 6 rooms, all ensuite. Fairly large estate built by Glasgow tobacco lord Robert Oswald, who reportedly had close connections with none other than Benjamin Franklin.

Kirkcudbright, *Gladstone House,* Gordon and Hilary Cowan, 48 High Street. Telephone/Fax: 01557-331734. E-mail: hilarygladstone@aol.com. Web site: www.kirkcudbrightgladstone.co.uk. 3 rooms, 2 ensuite, 1 with shower only. Georgian townhouse near the harbor, castle, art galleries, and restaurants. Afternoon teas are served in the elegant drawing room or secluded garden. No smoking.

Kirkcudbright, *1 Gordon Place,* Heather Black, High Street. Telephone: 01557-330472. 2 rooms with private facilities. Immaculately clean 200-year-old house opposite Broughton House. Very lovely.

Kirkpatrick Fleming, *The Mill,* Kathleen M. Smith, Grahamshill. Telephone: 01461-800344 or 01461-800603. Fax: 01461-800255. 24 rooms, all ensuite. Converted farmstead built circa 1750. Located in a tranquil setting on the outskirts of Gretna Green.

Moffat, *Alba House,* Evelyn Lindsay, 20 Beechgrove. Telephone/Fax: 01683-220418. 2 rooms, both ensuite. Built circa 1730. Boasts a beamed dining room with inglenook. A few minutes' walk from town center.

Moffat, *Boleskine,* Sheila and Andy Armstrong, 4 Well Road. Telephone: 01683-220601. 4 rooms, 2 ensuite. The Armstrongs are a friendly couple who do their best to make you feel at home at their large Victorian house. Located on a quiet street a few minutes' walk from the town center. Good and healthy home cooking served.

Moniaive, *Park House,* Mrs. Bradley, Dunreggan. Telephone: 01848-200440. 2 rooms with private facilities. Artist-run family home located on the edge of historic Moniaive. Home baking their specialty.

New Abbey, *Criffel Inn,* 2 The Square, by Dumfries. Telephone: 01387-850305. 5 rooms, 4 ensuite. Family-run hotel in the pretty village of New Abbey. A short walk away from the evocatively romantic ruins of Sweetheart Abbey. Sandy beaches, golf, and sea angling opportunities also nearby.

Edinburgh

In 1999 the Scottish Parliament returned to Edinburgh, a momentous occasion in the history of a country that has seen more than its share of triumphant as well as disastrous events. But the new Parliament seems to have rekindled a long-smoldering spirit of hope and optimism in this most famous of Scottish cities.

Despite the controversy surrounding it (it was three years late and millions of pounds—it cost £431 million or more than $760 million—over budget), the Scottish Parliament building has become Edinburgh's latest tourist attraction since officially opening in September 2004. You either love or hate it, though. Within a space of a few minutes, I overheard one local sniff, "I'm not impressed" while another, a visiting American no less, gushed, "Is this cool or what? That is neat."

The late Barcelonian architect Enric Miralles won an international competition to design the building. Whatever you think of it, it certainly is eye-catching. The complex consists of the Debating Chamber, a mostly steel-framed building clad in concrete panels and four tower buildings, which feature panels of oak, gray, and black granite. Perhaps the complex's most unusual features though are the roofs, which are shaped like upturned boats and are covered in stainless steel. Meanwhile, the MSP Building, six stories at its highest point, is constructed from a series of concrete units and its exterior is clad in a variety of materials, including South African granite.

The most moving aspect of the entire complex, though, must be the Canongate Wall. Set into the wall are stones from throughout Scotland, many with quotations cut into them. Some quotations are from the Bible (Psalm 19), some are Gaelic proverbs ("Say but little . . . and say it well"), and others are thoughts from writers and poets (Robert Burns and Robert Louis Stevenson, but also contemporaries such as poet Edwin Morgan and novelist Alasdair Gray). A guided tour costs £3.50 for adults, £1.75 for seniors.

If you're curious about what goes on behind the scenes, you can arrange to watch the Parliament in action on business days (generally

Tuesday-Thursday from 9 A.M. to 7 P.M.) But you must book in advance. For further information, phone (0131) 348-5000 or check the web site at www.scottish.parliament.uk.

Part of this new spirit can also be seen in the fairly new—it opened in late 1998—Museum of Scotland, which contains the history of Scotland all under one roof, from its geological beginnings to the waning days of the twentieth century. The handsome structure, with its modified turret, acknowledges the past as it nods to the future.

Edinburgh is also a city of culture, from the almost embarrassing riches that comprise the Edinburgh International Festival each August to the daily diet of theater, nightlife, and fine restaurants that beckons both visitor and resident alike throughout the rest of the year.

Most visitors to this handsome city will undoubtedly spend most of their time in the Old Town and the New Town. In Edinburgh, what constitutes "old" and "new" is relative. In this case, the Old Town, or the Royal Mile, as it is also known, refers to the area, actually more than a mile in length, which stretches from brooding Edinburgh Castle to the Palace of Holyrood. This Royal Mile captures the spirit of another, darker era, of narrow passageways and dank tenements, of thievery and debauchery, and of lives lived in the shadow of crime and disease.

Fortunately, conditions have brightened considerably since then. Of course, the castle is a must. But other highlights include the Scotch Whisky Heritage Centre, where you'll learn more about Scotland's national drink than you ever thought possible; the Writer's Museum, a collection of memorabilia dedicated to that Caledonian trio of letters—Robert Burns, Sir Walter Scott, and Robert Louis Stevenson; the wonder of St. Giles Cathedral; as well as many other small museums, arts centers, coffeehouses, historic pubs, and old inns.

The New Town, on the other hand, was built in the eighteenth century. It's a genteel corner of the city consisting of elegant townhouses fronting parks, squares, and circles. Everything in the New Town exudes harmony, serenity, and reason, a sense of exquisite balance and an overall good feeling that all is right with the world.

Edinburgh's premier shopping street is Princes Street. Although probably not as significant as it once was, it is still a fine thoroughfare, lined with old-fashioned hotels and department stores, bookstores, and all kinds of shops, from tourist tacky to the subtly elegant. Across the street is the open expanse of the Princes Street Gardens. When the crowds become overwhelming it's reassuring to know that you're only a few steps away from a leafy haven.

Of the many cultural institutions that await you in Edinburgh, you should at least consider visiting the National Gallery of Scotland, the Scottish National Portrait Gallery, the Scottish National Gallery of Modern Art, and the Traverse Theatre, to name but a few.

Balmoral Guest House
Marc Pimbert
32 Pilrig Street
Edinburgh
Telephone: 0131-554-1857
Fax: 0131-553-5712
E-mail: marc@balmoralguesthouse.co.uk
Web site: www.balmoralguesthouse.co.uk
Bedrooms: 5, 1 ensuite, 2 with showers immediately outside.
Rates: £40-45 double. **Credit cards:** VISA and MasterCard. **Open:** Year-round. **Children:** Yes. **Pets:** Guide dogs only. **Smoking:** No. **Provision for handicapped:** Limited. **Directions:** Take bus number 10, 11, 12, 16, 22, or 25 from Princes Street and get off at Pilrig Church.

This small family guesthouse is located in a Victorian townhouse built in 1856 and is located along a pleasant residential street less than a mile from Waverley Station. All the rooms are furnished with period furniture. Marc offers a full Scottish breakfast. He also caters to vegetarians.

40A Heriot Row
Diane and Robert Rae
40A Heriot Row
Edinburgh
Telephone: 0131-226-2068
Fax: 0131-225-6266
E-mail: enquiries@heriotrow.com
Bedrooms: 2 rooms, ensuite.
Rates: £60 single and £100 double. **Credit cards:** No. **Open:** Year-round. **Children:** Yes. **Pets:** No. **Smoking:** Restricted. **Provision for handicapped:** No. **Directions:** Located in the New Town, across from Queen Street Gardens.

The Raes run a lovely bed and breakfast in their smartly elegant New Town townhouse with great panache, style, and charm. Robert, a native of Edinburgh, is tall, bearded, and urbane, a perfect gentleman; Diane is from south of the Border, warm and conversational with no airs or pretenses about her. Each proves to be the perfect foil for the other, as well as being endlessly entertaining to their guests. The cozy and snug bedrooms are located in the lower level, safely ensconsced from the noise and hassle of the outside world. Breakfast is served in the book-lined dining room and can range from the simple (muesli, fresh fruit, toast, and tea or coffee) to the extravagant (a Sunday champagne brunch of smoked salmon and eggs, for example, or a plate of kippers and sometimes a slice of haggis). Guests have access to a hair dryer, shoe cleaning equipment, a clothes brush, complimentary body lotions and shampoos, and other little personal touches. The Raes make friends easily; once you have been here, you will want to return again and again.

Hawes Inn

David and Caroline MacGregor
7 Newhalls Road
South Queensferry
Edinburgh
Telephone: 0131-331-1990
Web site: www.innkeeperslodge.com
Bedrooms: All ensuite.
Rates: £39.95-79.95 per room. **Credit cards:** Delta, MasterCard, American Express, Switch, VISA. **Open:** Year-round. **Children:** Yes. **Pets:** No. **Smoking:** Yes. **Provision for handicapped:** No. **Directions:** From the M8, follow signs for the Forth Road Bridge. Exit at Junction Two onto the M9, which then becomes the A8000. At the roundabout take the B907 and follow until the junction with the B924. Turn right at Newhalls Road.

This handsomely picturesque inn with a friendly, village pub atmosphere—nooks and crannies, antique photographs, wooden tables and chairs—was immortalized by Robert Louis Stevenson and, before him, Sir Walter Scott in *The Antiquary*. Stevenson stayed here in 1886, in Room 13 (the number has since been changed to Room 7); two chapters from his classic novel *Kidnapped* are set at the Hawes Inn. In his essay "A Gossip of Romance," he described it as being "apart from the town, beside the pier, in a climate of its own, half inland, half marine—in front, the ferry bubbling with the tide and the guard—ship swinging to her anchor; behind, the old garden with the trees."

The centuries-old whitewashed inn—it dates back to 1683—is located across from the Forth Rail Bridge in the historic and charming town of South Queensferry. Outside hangs a sign that features one of Stevenson's characters and a number of the rooms are named after figures from his works, such as the David Balfour Room. In fact, Stevenson's presence is most everywhere here. You can have a meal in the Robert Louis Stevenson Room, for example, accompanied by a small bust of the author, looking stylish with a cravat around his neck, along with Stevenson photographs, etchings, and, of course, copies of his books. For a literary souvenir, RLS tea towels go for £3 each. Although run by the MacGregor family, the Hawes Inn is owned by Innkeeper's Lodge, a nationwide chain that operates vintage inns throughout Britain. South Queensferry itself is a charming village of cobblestone streets, colorful cottages, and historic pubs. It's only a 15-minute journey by train from Edinburgh.

The Dalmeny railway station is a short walk—about a quarter-mile from the inn. While in South Queensferry, don't miss the history museum on the main road that has a fascinating display on the Ferry Festival, a local custom associated with good fortune, and its most fascinating feature, the Burry Man of South Queensferry. Each year a resident of the town is chosen to be the Burry Man, a sort of fertility figure. Clad from head to ankle in burrs (it takes up to 2 hours to dress him), he is paraded through the streets. The museum displays a life-size figure of the Burry Man.

22 Murrayfield Gardens
Tim and Christine MacDowel
22 Murrayfield Gardens
Edinburgh
Telephone: 0131-337-3569
E-mail: mac@number22.co.uk
Web site: www.number22.co.uk
Bedrooms: 3, all ensuite or with private facilities.
Rates: £40-45 double. **Credit cards:** MasterCard, VISA. **Open:** Year-round except Christmas. **Children:** Yes. **Pets:** Yes, by arrangement. **Smoking:** No. **Provision for handicapped:** Limited. **Directions:** One mile west of Edinburgh city center, just off the A8. Murrayfield Gardens runs north from A8, 150 yards west of Roseburn Terrace.

This charming Victorian sandstone house stands amid its own grounds and is located in a quiet part of Edinburgh yet still only one mile from Princes Street. Both airport buses and regular city buses pass within 300 yards of the house. It's about a 10-minute journey into the city center. Each room is individually furnished. Tim makes the breakfasts himself, everything from a continental breakfast (grapefruit, melon, home-baked croissants) to what he calls a "Full Monty" breakfast, which may consist of eggs, bacon, sausage, mushrooms, and tomatoes. Vegetarian breakfasts can also be arranged.

Stevenson House
Mrs. Macfie
17 Heriot Row
Edinburgh
Telephone/Fax: 0131-556-1896
E-mail: mail@stevenson-house.co.uk
Web site: www.stevenson-house.co.uk
Bedrooms: 3 rooms, 1 ensuite.
Rates: £45 single, £120 double. **Credit cards:** Yes. **Open:** Year-round.
Children: Yes. **Pets:** No. **Smoking:** No. **Provision for handicapped:** No.
Directions: Located in the New Town, across from Queen Street
Gardens.

As you approach the imposing front door of 17 Heriot Row, you
can't help but notice the sign above the doorbell: PRIVATE HOUSE NOT A
MUSEUM. How often does one get the chance to stay in the home of a
world-class author? Stevenson House was the childhood home of master storyteller Robert Louis Stevenson. Nothing seems to have
changed much within these walls. The atmosphere still reeks of
Victorian Edinburgh—dimly lit rooms and a reserved tranquility that
is far removed from the noise of the twenty-first century world that lies
outside its doors.

The double bedroom on the first floor was the bedroom of
Stevenson's parents, Thomas and Maggie. It features a four-poster bed
and William Morris-pattern wallpaper. Two single rooms are on the
second floor—both share a bathroom. One is located at the back and
offers a view across to Fife, the other, at the front of the building, is
Stevenson's actual bedroom. Stevenson loved the sound of horses'
hoofs on the old Edinburgh streets. With a little imagination, you can
too. Appropriately, a small bust of the writer stands atop a sideboard in
the hallway, welcoming you into his former abode. Given that
Stevenson House is a literary and cultural landmark, rates here are
surprisingly modest.

The Witchery by the Castle
James Thomson
Castlehill
The Royal Mile
Edinburgh
Telephone: 0131-225-5613
Fax: 0131-220-4392
Web site: www.thewitchery.com
Bedrooms: 6 suites, all with private facilities.
Rates: Room rate from £275 per night. **Credit cards:** Yes. **Open:** Year-round. **Children:** Yes. **Pets:** No. **Smoking:** In restaurant. **Provision for handicapped:** No. **Directions:** Located at the top of the Royal Mile close to Edinburgh Castle in the heart of the Old Town. Parking is available at the nearby NCP car park on Castle Terrace.

This Edinburgh landmark is so special and, admittedly, so decadent, that it properly belongs in a category all by itself. Edinburgh native James Thomson founded the Witchery restaurant in 1979 in what was then a crumbling 16th-century building. Ten years later, he added the Secret Garden, a cozy restaurant annex that was built on the site of an adjacent derelict schoolyard that once housed a witches' coven. And then, in 1991, he created a series of opulent suites on floors above the restaurant, first the Inner Sanctum, then the Old Rectory, and, in 2003, several new suites. First and foremost, though, the Witchery is a restaurant. But not just any restaurant. It is one of the best—some say *the* best—in Edinburgh.

A typical menu might consist of a starter of small steak tartare, a main course of grilled filet of Scotch beef or confit of wild salmon or roasted sea bass, and dessert of peach melba or chocolate torte or passion fruit and raspberry mousse. Entrees range from £14.95 to £29.95. Sleeping here comes at a price too. The Witchery's 6 suites are luxurious, the ultimate in indulgence, and have been named among Britain's most romantic destinations *(Cosmopolitan* magazine went so far as to call the Witchery suites one of the world's Seven Wonders—granted, an exaggeration, but not by much). For a hefty £275 (and up) per night, you get antique-filled suites that feature a Bose sound system, CDs, videos, a collection of books, and cable television. They also come with a continental breakfast, chocolates, mineral water, newspapers, and a complimentary bottle of Pol Roger Champagne.

The Inner Sanctum suite features a leather sofa and wing chairs and a large lacquer red bathroom with a Victorian roll-top bath for two. The baroque Old Rectory suite has oak paneled and red fabric- covered walls.

The lavish bed was created from an antique pulpit, and gilded bookcases flank the marble fireplace. A small dressing room leads to the mirrored and gilded-wall bathroom with its painted vaulted ceiling. The Library suite overlooks the Royal Mile and lives up to its name with its book-lined bathroom and a bath for two. The gothic Vestry suite is decorated in a dramatic black, red, and gold color scheme. The Armoury suite overlooks a small private courtyard and is hung with various tapestries and features an oak-paneled bathroom. The spacious Guardroom suite overlooks the rooftops of Edinburgh's Old Town and boasts an antique leathered bedroom.

The Witchery's location, at the top of the Royal Mile within hailing distance of Edinburgh Castle, can't be beat. If you do choose to dine and stay here, you would have had plenty of fine company. Famous customers have included Jack Nicholson, Michael Douglas and Catherine Zeta-Jones, Pierce Brosnan, and Ewan McGregor. By all means, come around Halloween when the Witchery is at its spookiest, but don't forget it the rest of the year either. Just remember to bring along a very thick wallet.

ALSO RECOMMENDED

Edinburgh, *17A Abercromby Place,* Eirlys Lloyd, 17 Abercromby Place. Telephone: 0131-557-8036. Fax: 0131-558-3453. E-mail: eiryls.lloyd@virgin.net. 9 rooms, all ensuite. Historic Georgian house; formerly the home of Edinburgh architect William Playfair. Handsome, elegant, the epitome of New Town style. Two of the nicest rooms are located on the upper floor at the back of the main house. Comfortable dining room and sitting rooms too. Generally rates range from £45-50 per person.

Edinburgh, *Castle Guest House,* 38 Castle Street North. Telephone/Fax: 0131-225-1975. E-mail: info@castleguesthouse.com. Tod and Pauline Hetherington. 7 rooms, all ensuite. Located in the center of Edinburgh in a Georgian building that was constructed in 1792. The Hetheringtons have completely renovated it. Several literary touches add to the charm. An exterior plaque reminds visitors that Kenneth Grahame, author of *The Wind in the Willows,* was born in this building in March 1859. From the breakfast room, visitors can also see the house where Sir Walter Scott lived from 1802 to 1826. Rates range from £35-45 per person.

Edinburgh, *Channings,* Peter and Mhairi Taylor, South Learmonth Gardens. Telephone: 0131-315-2226. Fax: 0131-332-9631. 48 rooms, all ensuite. A combination of five Edwardian townhouses on a quiet cobblestoned street in the New Town. Relaxed ambiance. Channings also houses the Brasserie, a fine restaurant of Scottish and French cooking.

Edinburgh, *The Christopher North Hotel,* 6 Gloucester Place. Telephone: 0131-225-2720. Fax: 0131-220-4706. E-mail reservations@christopher-north.co.uk. Web site: www.christophernorth.co.uk. An elegant, sophisticated boutique hotel with a Continental feel that was once the home of Christopher North, the pen name of Scottish essayist, poet, writer, and editor John Wilson. Wilson was a founder of *Blackwood's Magazine* and taught philosophy at Edinburgh University. A historic plaque notes that he lived here from 1826 to 1854. All rooms are ensuite and start at £68 single and £98 double.

Edinburgh, *Dene Guest House,* 7 Eyre Place. Telephone: 0131-556-2700. Fax: 0131-557-9876. Charming Georgian townhouse in a good location at affordable rates.

Edinburgh, *Drummond House,* 17 Drummond Place. Telephone: 0131-225-1101. 3 rooms. New Town charmer with canopied beds and antique furniture.

Edinburgh, *4 Forres Street,* Billy and Yvonne McLellan. Telephone: 0131-220-5073. Fax: 0131-220-2660. E-mail: ForresStreet@aol.com. 5 rooms, all ensuite. 4 Forres Street does double duty: a guesthouse on the upper floors and a small children's day nursery on the ground floor. Some of the rooms are very spacious and come with king-sized four-poster bed and sitting-room area. One room even has a Jacuzzi with underwater lighting. Prices range from £45-60 per person.

Edinburgh, *7 Gloucester Place,* Naomi Jennings. Telephone: 0131-225-2974. E-mail: naomijennings@hotmail.com. 3 rooms, 1 ensuite, 1 with private bathroom, 1 with shower room nearby. The B&B is located on the top two floors in a building that dates back to the early nineteenth century. Naomi speaks a smattering of French and Italian and serves a full Scottish breakfast or a lighter Continental one—depending on the preferences of her guests. She runs the place with the help of her pointer, Quail. Rates range from £30-45 double.

Edinburgh, *50 India Street,* Sandra and John Keith. Telephone: 0131-225-3340. E-mail: sandrakeith@brilliantbreakfasts.com. 1 room, with private shower. 50 India Street is located on a quiet cobble-stoned cul-de-sac across from the Royal Circus Gardens. Sandra, originally from Glasgow, is friendly and gregarious. Her cheery home is decorated with antiques and modern artwork, including oil paintings by her own daughter. An avid traveler, Sandra is known for her organic breakfasts; some dishes have a slightly Mediterranean flavor. Whenever possible, she uses produce from local farmers and suppliers. A single here costs £55, a double £95.

Edinburgh, *24 Northumberland Street,* 24 Northumberland Street. Telephone: 0131-556-8140.   Fax: 0131-556-4423.   E-mail: ingram@ednet.co.uk. 3 rooms, most ensuite. Classic Georgian townhouse a few minutes' walk from Princes Street and Waverley Station. Features period decoration with antique furnishings.

Edinburgh, *Six Mary's Place,* Raeburn Place. Douglas Tully, manager. Telephone: 0131-332-8965. Fax: 0131-624-7060. E-mail: info@six-marysplace.co.uk. 8 rooms, 7 ensuite, 1 with private bathroom. Situated in a trendy part of Edinburgh and only a short walk or bus ride from Princes Street and the Royal Mile. Features a vegetarian breakfast, including vegetarian sausages and (for the adventurous) vegetarian haggis. Rates are affordable too—£30-48 per person. And unlike many B&Bs, each room has an Internet connection, television, and telephone.

Edinburgh, *Turret Guest House,* Jackie and Ian Cameron, 8 Kilmaurs Terrace. Telephone: 0131-667-6704. Fax: 0131-668-1368. 3 rooms. This Victorian guesthouse is located in a quiet part of town. Among its notable features are a wooden staircase, attractive and neat bedrooms, and unusual breakfasts (haggis has been known to appear on the menu).

Fife

"The Kingdom of Fife" has a nice ring to it. More than just an attractive moniker though, the name signifies the important position that the region held in earlier times, first as the seat of early Celtic kings in Dunfermline and later as the ecclesiastical capital in St. Andrews.

Nowadays most people associate Fife not with dead monarchs and clerics but rather with golf, charming fishing villages, and a great and ancient university.

The list of attractions to see and things to do in St. Andrews is considerable. Founded in 1410-11, St. Andrews University is the oldest university in Scotland—its buildings are scattered throughout the town, and students offer guided tours of the university during the summer months.

For many years St. Andrews was considered an important center of pilgrimage. St. Andrews Museum offers a solid introduction to the city's ecclesiastical, academic, and civic history, as well as a fascinating exhibit on the medieval pilgrims. After digesting the historical highlights, make your way to the ruins of St. Andrews Cathedral and the 100-foot St. Rule's Tower.

Of course, St. Andrews wouldn't be St. Andrews without golf. Every golfer's dream is to play at the Royal and Ancient Golf Club, the home of golf. If your skill level doesn't quite match your ambition, no matter. You can learn everything you've always wanted to know about golf—and more—at the very informative British Golf Museum. Of course, it's only a few steps from the Royal and Ancient.

In Fife the sea is never too far away. Discover its maritime history at the Scottish Fisheries Museum in Anstruther. Or better yet get a taste of the sea itself by visiting the East Neuk of Fife, which consists of a string of attractive fishing villages from Earlsferry to Crail. Further south in tiny Dysart sits a cluster of seventeenth-century fisher houses, complete with crowstep gables, that huddle around the picturesque old harbor.

Inland Fife has its share of attractive villages too, such as tony Falkland. My vote for the prettiest village in the area, though, goes to

Culross (pronounced "COO-rus"), with its red roofs and narrow cob-blestoned streets. Although it may look like a museum piece, it really is a viable community. You could easily spend an entire day here exploring the nooks and crannies of the village or visiting the numer-ous museums and historic buildings. Don't forget to stop by the impressive thirteenth-century Culross Abbey.

The Smugglers Inn
Ian Lowson
High Street
Anstruther
Telephone: 01333-310506
Fax: 01333-312706
E-mail: smugglers@foxinns.com
Web site: www.foxinns.com
Bedrooms: 8 rooms, all ensuite.
Rates: £30-45 singles, £45-75 double. **Credit cards:** VISA, MasterCard, Switch, Solo. **Open:** Year-round. **Children:** Well-behaved children are welcome regardless of age. **Pets:** By arrangement. **Smoking:** Yes, but courtesy is expected. **Provision for handicapped:** No. **Directions:** From Edinburgh go to dual carriageway joining the M90. Exit the M90 at Junction 2 (Kirkcaldy-Glenrothes). Stay on this road until you come to a roundabout. Take the third exit (City Centre-St. Andrews). Continue on this road until you reach the village of Anstruther. The inn is situated on the right just past the "bad bend."

The original inn dates back to 1300. In the days of Queen Anne, during the eighteenth century, it functioned as a tavern and even had some historical associations with the Jacobite Rising of 1715. The inn overlooks the harbor on the River Forth and is surrounded by some of the best golf courses in Scotland, as well as many fine beaches. Pleasantly decorated, it offers a comfy lounge with log fires. The neat and attractive whitewashed building with black trim sports a rustic look. Now run by the Foxinns Group, a small company that specializes in rural and coastal hotels, the inn is managed by Ian Lowson, a native of the area who worked for the previous owners, Neil and Christine Park. If you have the time, wander along the old streets of Anstruther. A "must stop" is the Scottish Fisheries Museum on the harbor, which is housed in a cluster of historic buildings around a cobbled courtyard. This fine museum covers virtually all aspects of Scotland's fishing history, from fisherfolk life to fishing tragedies.

The Spindrift Guest House
Ken and Christine Lawson
Pittenweem Road
Anstruther
Telephone/Fax: 01333-310573
E-mail: info@thespindrift.co.uk
Web site: www.thesprindrift.co.uk
Bedrooms: 8, 7 ensuite and 1 with private bathroom.
Rates: £10 single, £27.50-38 pp. double. **Credit cards:** VISA,
MasterCard, Maestro, JCB, Solo, American Express. **Open:** Year-round
except Christmas and January. **Children:** 10 years and older. **Pets:** By
arrangement. **Smoking:** No. **Provision for handicapped:** No.
Directions: A 10-minute drive from St. Andrews.

This stone-built Victorian home is located in the fishing village of
Anstruther. Your hosts are Ken and Christine Lawson, who took over
from the previous owners in 2000. Guests can enjoy a pre-dinner drink
in the cozy lounge. A unique and popular feature is the Captain's
Room, on the top floor. The original owner of the house, a tea clipper
captain by the name of Captain Smith, made the room into the replica
of a ship master's cabin. Its east-facing window looks toward Anstruther,
where the captain could watch the tea clippers and the fishing fleet in
the harbor. The Lawsons also can help with golf tee times.

Caiplie Guest House
Finlay Kerr
53 High Street
Crail
Telephone/Fax: 01333-450564
Web site: www.caipliehouse.com
E-mail: mail@caipliehouse.com
Bedrooms: 6 rooms, 4 ensuite.
Rates: From £20-45 pp. **Credit cards:** None. **Open:** March-November.
Children: Yes. **Pets:** By arrangement. **Smoking:** Yes. **Provision for handicapped:** No. **Directions:** Located along Crail's main street, about 10 miles south of St. Andrews.

This comfortable and casual Victorian guesthouse is run by Finlay Kerr, who lives on the premises. Some of the rooms offer wonderful sea views. What's more, the very reasonable accommodations, combined with tasty home cooking, make this a great bargain. Another advantage is the guesthouse's enviable location in the heart of the atmospheric fishing village of Crail, the most easterly of the fishing villages located in the East Neuk of Fife. The town's stone-built vernacular architecture, red pantile roofs, steeped gables, and narrow winding streets are so characteristic of the area. Ask Finlay and the staff about things to do in the area. Best of all though, the Caiplie has an excellent reputation for good, home-cooked meals. Every meal is cooked to order.

Dundonald Arms Hotel
Michael Batchelor
Mid Causeway
Culross
Telephone/Fax: 01383-881137
Bedrooms: 7 rooms, all ensuite.
Rates: £40 per room (breakfast is extra here: a light breakfast goes for £4.50, a full breakfast for £7). **Credit cards:** VISA and MasterCard. **Open:** Year-round. **Children:** All ages. **Pets:** Restricted. **Smoking:** Yes. **Provision for handicapped:** Limited to ground floor. **Directions:** Located in the heart of Culross, which is located on the western edges of Fife.

The Dundonald is a grand old building located in the heart of the historic village of Culross. The present building dates back to 1640 and over the centuries has offered many a visitor shelter, food, and a wee dram. "Rumor has it," says Michael, the proprietor, "that a few friendly spirits have remained from yesteryear; no doubt still enjoying the friendly company of today's visitors and the locals who use our bars for the odd refreshment." The Dundonald has two eating and drinking area. The Top Bar functions as the village's meeting area and has a nautical theme. It also has a fine selection of malt whiskies. Whisky is also the theme of the Quaich Lounge, and prints of old Culross decorate its walls.

Also on the premises is Jackie's Gift Shop. A piece of trivia: a tunnel passes under the gift shop floor that, in earlier times, was used by monks who lived in the village and later by smugglers. In good weather you can sit outside by the old Stables and relax, and dream if you wish, in this quiet and utterly charming part of Scotland. For those with more active interests, several golf courses are within a short drive, and sailing can be arranged at South Queensferry, about eight miles away. Whether you are staying overnight or just stopping by for a pint, the staff at the Dundonald Arms is unfailingly friendly and welcoming.

**The Albany Hotel &
Garden Restaurant**
Antonio and Celia Ferraro
56 North Street
St. Andrews
Telephone: 01334-477737
Fax: 01334-477742
Web site: www.standrewsalbany.co.uk
E-mail: mail@standrowsalbany.co.uk **Bedrooms:** 21 rooms, all ensuite.
Rates: £55 per person. **Credit cards:** MasterCard, VISA, Delta, Diners
Club, American Express, Switch. **Open:** Year-round. **Children:** Yes.
Pets: No. **Smoking:** In smoker's lounge only. **Provision for handicapped:** No. **Directions:** Located near the ruins of St. Andrews
Cathedral.

This Georgian townhouse, circa 1795, has been converted by the
Ferraros to a small family-run hotel. From the moment you arrive at
the Albany, you can't help but be won over by its combination of restful tranquility and a genuine effort to please its guests. It also doesn't
hurt that the owners have a wonderful sense of humor and, after 15
years of marriage, offer playful jabs at each other's expense for the
benefit of their guests. Antonio is originally from Naples, and Celia is
a native of St. Andrews. They met in Monte Carlo and eventually
made their way to St. Andrews, a fortunate circumstance for visitors
to the city. The rooms are bright, cheery, and clean. One room
called the Den, which faces away from street noise, has its own private garden and offers a soothing respite from the real world. There
is a resident's bar with log fire and small library. The on-premises
Garden Restaurant serves food with a Mediterranean flair. The
Ferraros can also help organize golf outings, nights at the theatre, or
tours of the area.

Aslar Guest House
Jean and Arlen Pardoe
120 North Street
St. Andrews
Telephone: 01334-473460
Fax: 01334-477540
E-mail: pardoe@aslar.u-net.com
Bedrooms: 5 rooms, all ensuite.
Rates: £25-30 pp. **Credit cards:** VISA and MasterCard. **Open:** Year-round. **Children:** All ages. **Pets:** No. **Smoking:** Restricted. **Provision for handicapped:** No. **Directions:** From Edinburgh take the road to the Forth Bridge/M90/A91. Follow the main road into St. Andrews, which becomes North Street.

The Pardoes started their career in the hospitality business in a modest way, back when their family was still young. Eventually they wished to try greater challenges, and so when an old house on North Street became available they "bit the bullet." The building dates from 1865 and was constructed on the site of a former coach house. Twenty years later it was purchased by a professor of Divinity and Biblical Criticism at nearby St. Andrews University. The Pardoes bought the property in 1985 and began major renovations, including removal of old and very heavy stone baths. It took several years for additional upgrading before Jean and Arlen were satisfied. ("We froze for the first winter without central heating," they say now.) The result is a comfortable and modern dwelling, but one that also retains vestiges of its considerable past. The Aslar is a charming place by any standard.

The Dunvegan Hotel

Jack and Sheena Willoughby
7 Pilmour Place
St. Andrews
Telephone: 01334-473105
Fax: 01334-479102
E-mail: dunveganhotel@easynet.co.uk
Web site: www.dunvegan-hotel.com
Bedrooms: 8, all ensuite.
Rates: £90-130 double. **Credit cards:** MasterCard, VISA, American
Express. **Open:** Year-round except January. **Children:** Yes. **Pets:** No.
Smoking: All bedrooms are non-smoking. **Provision for handicapped:**
No. **Directions:** The Dunvegan Hotel is located in the heart of town.

Whether you love golf or not, this is the place to be. Jack, a fourth
generation Texan, and Sheena, a native Scot from Forfar, are your
hosts. They and their staff offer friendly, personalized service. The
Dunvegan's lounge bar is decorated with more than 100 prints of historic and significant golfing scenes, including all the British Open win-
ners at St. Andrews dating back to Tom Kidd in 1873. The Claret Jug
restaurant is an informal dining room that specializes in char-grilled
steaks as well as chicken and fish dishes. For obvious reasons, golfers—
ordinary folk and famous alike—have a soft spot for the Dunvegan.
Curtis Strange, Fred Couples, John Daly, Nick Price, Ernie Els, and
Tiger Woods have stopped by. And not only golfers. Sean Connery,
Clint Eastwood, and George Herbert Walker Bush have also been
patrons. In 1999, Jack and Sheena acquired a 3 bedroom, 2 bathroom
flat above the famous Auchterlonie Golf Shop. It now goes by the
name of the Auchterlonie Suite and can sleep 6 golfers comfortably.

Glenderran Guest House
Ray and Maggie Pead
9 Murray Park
St. Andrews
Telephone: 01334-477951
Fax: 01334-477908
E-mail: glenderran@telinco.com
Bedrooms: 5 rooms, all ensuite.
Rates: £28-45 pp. **Credit cards:** Delta, VISA, MasterCard, Switch.
Open: Year-round. **Children:** Over 12. **Pets:** No. **Smoking:** No.
Provision for handicapped: No. **Directions:** Enter St. Andrews on the
A91 road. On entering town go straight over the first roundabout
and then straight over the next mini-roundabout (rather than turning
right). Turn into Murray Place, by the Tudor Inn. Follow the road
round and turn right into Murray Park (a one-way street).

This small late-Victorian guesthouse is centrally located just a few
hundred yards from the Old Course, beach, town center, and the university. It's run by Ray and Maggie Pead, a lovely couple, who specialize
in customized and friendly service. Consider some of their thoughtful
details: Individual bottles of mineral water are freshly supplied each day,
and in addition to the usual color remote-control television, they have
added a CD/cassette/radio player with a selection of CDs provided.
Each room is individually and tastefully decorated. Their largest
room, the Superior room, includes a three-seat sofa, 26-inch television
and video player, and such original Victorian features as elaborate ceiling work, marble fireplace, and bay windows. A full Scottish breakfast
or, for those with lighter appetites, a continental breakfast, is served.
There's always a selection of cheeses, smoked salmon with scrambled
egg, or vegetarian dishes on the menu. The dining room lounge is
perfect for relaxing and meeting with friends or having a drink.
There's also a good range of single malts, as well as a selection of
books, CDs, and board and card games.

Montague House
Jane and Ian
21 Murray Park
St. Andrews
Telephone: 01334-479287
Fax: 01334-475827
E-mail: info@montaguehouse.com
Web site: www.montaguehouse.com
Bedrooms: 7 rooms on 3 floors, all ensuite.
Rates: £30 pp. **Credit cards:** VISA, MasterCard. **Open:** February-November. **Children:** Yes. **Pets:** Yes. **Smoking:** Non-smoking bedrooms; smoking in lounge only. **Provision for handicapped:** No. **Directions:** Murray Park is a one-way street located off St. Andrews' main road.

This modernized Victorian terrace is located in the heart of town, minutes away from the Old Course. Rooms are individually decorated, with beautiful murals located throughout the house. Breakfasts at Montague House are special occasions, from a traditional Scottish breakfast to more unusual items such as pancakes (a rare breakfast item in Scotland) and seasonal fruit and yogurt.

The murals truly set the Montague apart. Each room is unique: five contain hand-painted murals and trompe l'eoil work done by local artist Gregor Gall; the nautically-themed Beachcomber has portholes painted on the walls; smothered in antique golf prints, the Bunker features a handpainted shelf on the wall and golf tees, sweets, and things painted on the window ledge; the Conservatory has an "amazing" ceiling that is painted like the sky; and the Secret Garden is a small but pretty pink room. The previous owners painted a garden in the dummy window and installed a window seat. Although Ceol-na-mara, the largest room with its king- and queen-size beds, has no murals, it does offer a Scottish theme in soothing plum colors. There is also a view of the East Neuk mural in the lounge and another mural on the half landing. The Montague is fully licensed, so drinks from the bar can be brought to your room.

The Peat Inn
David and Patricia Wilson
Cupar
Telephone: 01334-840206
Fax: 01334-840530
E-mail: reception@thepeatinn.co.uk
Web site: www.thepeatinn.co.uk
Bedrooms: 8 luxury suites
Rates: £95 single, £165 double. **Credit cards:** All major credit cards.
Open: Year-round. **Children:** Pets: **Smoking:** Yes. **Provision for handicapped:** No. **Directions:** Located 6 miles from St. Andrews.

For such a famous establishment, the Peat Inn has very modest beginnings. Originally an old coaching inn, it is now considered one of the finest restaurants in Britain. David Wilson's cooking has won countless accolades—in 1986, he was made a Chef Laureate by the British Gastronomic Academy. Continental breakfast consists of freshly squeezed orange juice, fruit compote, boiled egg, cheese, hot croissant, toast, tea or coffee. The rooms themselves have a sitting room with color television, writing desk, magazines, games, fresh fruit, and Scottish mineral water and are decorated with French period furniture. The bathrooms have Italian marble throughout.

Aside from the luxurious setting, it is the food that makes the Peat Inn distinctive. Lunch consists of 3 courses for £22; dinner is a 3-course set menu at £32. A 6-course tasting men is also available at £48. Among the dishes that have given the Peat Inn its enviable reputation for fine dining include filet of halibut on vegetable cake with potato gnocchi and herb sauce, medallions of monkfish and lobster with asparagus and wild mushroom in lobster sauce, and roast saddle of venison with a mushroom and truffle crust.

ALSO RECOMMENDED

Crail, *Selcraig House,* Margaret Carstairs, 47 Nethergate. Telephone: 01333-450697. 5 rooms. Centuries-old stone house, warm and relaxing, with Edwardian theme. Small garden in the back.

Dunfermline, *Clarke Cottage Guest House,* Aileen Neill, 139 Halbeath Road. Telephone: 01383-735935. clarkecottage@ukonline.co.uk. 9 rooms, all ensuite. This handsome nineteenth-century Victorian stone house is close to the town center. Guests can enjoy a separate entrance as well as ample off-street parking.

Dysart, *White Gates,* Tim and Ellis Musson, 91 Norman Road. Telephone: 01592-653337. 2 rooms; 1 ensuite, 1 shared. Victorian house with spacious bedrooms in the historic and lovely town of Dysart.

Kingsbarns, *Cambo House,* Mr. P. Erskine. Telephone: 01333-450313. Fax: 01333-450987. 2 rooms, 1 ensuite. Wooded coastal estate near St. Andrews. Features gardens, grounds, and fourposter beds; near woodlands and sandy beaches.

Kirkcaldy, *Arboretum,* Elizabeth Duncan, 20 Southerton Road. Telephone: 01592-643673. 2 rooms, both ensuite. Extended bungalow overlooking leafy Beveridge Park. Short walk to rail and bus stations and town center.

Leslie, *The Coach House,* David Morrison, Auchmuirbridge, near Glenrothes. Telephone/Fax: 01592-744934. 4 rooms, all ensuite. Beautiful white stucco home with red-tiled roof in a lovely part of rural Fife. Comfortably furnished, there are also plenty of outdoor activities to choose from: walking on the Lomond Hills, golf, shooting, fishing, and horseback riding.

Markinch, *Gamekeeper's Cottage,* Sam and Lesley Millar, Balbirnie Park. Telephone: 01592-612742. 2 rooms, both ensuite. Original gamekeeper's cottage. Gamekeeper's is known for its delicious home cooking. The motto of the Millars is simple: "Drive Carefully, Get Here Safely, and We'll Do the Rest." What more could you ask for?

By **Markinch,** *Shythrum Farm,* Mrs. C. Craig. Telephone: 01592-758372. 2 rooms, 1 ensuite. Small B&B with red slate roof and plenty of historic charm.

St. Andrews, *Annandale Guest House,* Brian and Florence McAndie, 23 Murray Park. Telephone/Fax: 01334-475310. 5 rooms, all ensuite. Lovely Victorian house. Golf times can be arranged.

Near **St. Andrews,** *Little Carron Cottage,* Mrs. A. Finn, Little Carron Gardens. Telephone: 01334-474039. Fax: 01334-474039. 3 rooms, all ensuite. Attractive converted farmhouse in rural area. Each room has its own private lounge. Quiet, informal, friendly atmosphere. Excellent breakfasts.

St. Andrews, *11 Queens Gardens,* Muriel Gray. Telephone: 01334-475536. 3 rooms, 1 ensuite. Elegant Victorian family home in the heart of the historic center of town. Attractive bedrooms. All major attractions within walking distance.

Grampian

Castles, malt whisky trails, and fishing villages are just some of the better-known attractions of rural Grampian. Add to this the urban site of Aberdeen, Scotland's great maritime city, and you have an unusual combination. The Northeast also boasts a very rich folk tradition, from the colorful local dialects to the old ballads that are so greatly associated with this part of Scotland.

Aberdeen is the third-largest city in Scotland and, by dint of the silver granite buildings, one with an unusually distinctive look and feel. From Provost Skene's House, the oldest house in Aberdeen, to the icicle-like spires of magnificent Marischal College, Aberdeen looks like no other city in Scotland.

Founded as a royal burgh in 1124, Aberdeen developed into an important maritime center from its earliest days. You can discover more about its seaworthy past at the Aberdeen Maritime Museum, which explores everything from the days of the old clipper ships to the current spate of activity associated with the burgeoning oil industry. If you have time, try to visit lovely Old Aberdeen, a compact neighborhood of old stone cottages and cobblestoned streets and home to the campus of the University of Aberdeen. Several fine old churches are also here, including King's College Chapel and St. Machar's Cathedral. And don't forget the city's lively nightlife. Seek out the Lemon Tree for the latest sounds.

Rural Aberdeenshire is a world apart from the bustle of Aberdeen. It is a region of rolling hills, miles upon miles of woodland, and farming communities. The landscape is surprisingly diverse, from the fertile red soil of the interior to evocative fishing villages, including St. Cyrus, Johnshaven, Gourdon, and Stonehaven. While here you must order fish and chips at the Bervie Chipper in Inverbervie, a bustling and popular spot that has won numerous dining awards. Indeed, more than a few people insist that the Chipper serves the best fish and chips in Britain. I'll leave that distinction up to you.

Vast portions of Grampian seem terribly remote. The road to Braemar is as wild as any Highland glen. Royal Deeside, a favorite haunt of the royal family since Queen Victoria "discovered" the area in the 1840s, consists of delightful villages—pleasant Banchory, pretty Ballater, and subtly elegant Braemar.

And then there's the Malt Whisky Trail—Glenfarclas, Glenfiddich, Glenlivet, Macallan, Tamnavulin. Some of the names may sound familiar; others less so. Many of the distilleries have visitor's centers and offer free "wee drams." Proceed with caution though, especially if you're the driver.

Schiehallion House
Julie and Steven Heyes
10 Glenshee Road
Braemar
Telephone: 01339-741679
Bedrooms: 9 rooms, 5 ensuite.
Rates: £19-23 pp. **Credit cards:** MasterCard, VISA. **Open:** February-mid-September. **Children:** No. **Pets:** By arrangement. **Smoking:** In guest lounge only. **Provision for handicapped:** No. **Directions:** From the Mews in the village center, turn right. At road junction go south on A93 for 300 meters. Schiehallion is on the right.

This small stone-built B&B in the pretty village of Braemar is an all-family affair and a short walk from the village center. Schiehallion operates under the caring and watchful eyes of Julie and Steve and Steve's parents Sheila and Fred. The Heyes moved from the north of England to Braemar in June 1995 to "get away from the rat race," as they say. Steve and Julie cook the hearty breakfasts. Packed lunches are available on request. The rooms are attractive and the resident's lounge welcoming with its open fire. The village itself is a wonderful base for exploring the surrounding countryside. Within a short drive of the B&B are such attractions as Balmoral Castle, the royal family's summer quarters since the days of Queen Victoria; the wild delights of the Cairngorm Mountains; and a series of charming villages along the A93 from Ballater to Banchory. Don't miss the chance to explore Braemar itself, which is an utterly delightful village with many quality shops. The Braemar Gallery, for example, specializes in Scottish art, paintings, sculptures, etchings, and drawings.

ALSO RECOMMENDED

Aberdeen, *Aberdeen Springdale Guest House,* James Stirling, 404 Great Western Road. Telephone: 01224-316561. Fax: 0124-210773. E-mail: jamesestirling@msn.com. Web site: www.aberdeenguesthouse.co.uk. 6 rooms, some with private facilities. Warm and cozy Victorian house with spacious rooms. Great room rates too! Only £24-35 single, £20-25 double.

Ballater, *The Green Inn Restaurant with Rooms,* Trevor and Evelyn O'Halloran, 9 Victoria Road. Telephone: 013397-55701. Fax: 013997-56357. 3 rooms, all ensuite. The Green Inn is located in the center of the village, overlooking the village green. This two-story granite building offers modern Scottish cooking with international touches prepared to utmost perfection in its intimate dining room. All rooms have been upgraded by new owners Trevor and Evelyn O'Halloran. They have also added a conservatory with wood-burning stove.

Ballater, *Netherley Guest House,* Mrs. Jennifer Shand, 2 Netherley Place. Telephone: 013397-55792. E-mail: jennifer@shand.wanadoo.co.uk. 7 rooms, all ensuite. Pretty guesthouse overlooking Ballater's village green.

Elgin, *The Croft,* 10 Institution Road. Ann and Richard Cartmell. Telephone/Fax: 01343-546004. E-mail: thecroftelgin@hotmail.com. 3 rooms, 2 ensuite and 1 with private bathroom. Set in formal gardens, this Victorian house was built in 1848 for a local town clerk by the name of Patrick Duff. It is a short walk from Elgin Cathedral. Non-smoking.

Johnshaven, *The Retreat,* Christine Hulton, South Street. Telephone: 01561-362731. 2 rooms, 1 ensuite. Tranquility by the sea. The tiny fishing village of Johnshaven is undeniably delightful all its own. Everything here is on a small scale, which seems only right.

GLASGOW & STRATHCLYDE

Loch Lomond

CAMPSIE FELLS

Firth of Clyde

Gourock
Greenock
Dumbarton
Bearsden
Milngavie
Kirkintilloch
Cumbernauld
Port Glasgow
Clydebank
Bishopbriggs
Wemyss Bay
Renfrew
Stepps
Airdrie
Glasgow
Coatbridge
Paisley
Rutherglen
Bellshill
Largs
Uddingston
Motherwell
Hamilton
GREAT CUMBRAE
East Kilbride
LITTLE CUMBRAE
West Kilbride
Lanark
Ardrossan
Stevenston
New Lanark
Biggar
Saltcoats
Irvine
Kilmarnock
Darvel
Troon
Galston
Prestwick
Mauchline
Ayr
Tarbolton
Auchinleck
Alloway
Cumnock
New Cumnock
Maybole
Dalmellington
Kirkoswald
Turnberry
Girvan
Barr
Ballantrae
Barrhill

N

0   10 miles
0   10 kilometers

STRATHCLYDE
GLASGOW

Glasgow & Strathclyde

If you had told a native of Glasgow a dozen or so years ago that the "dear green place," the city's nickname, would be in the throes of a major cultural renaissance, you would have been treated with wails of delirious laughter.

Who's laughing now?

Make no mistake about it: Scotland's largest city is enjoying a cultural epiphany unlike anything it has experienced in its history. Ever since it won the coveted European City of Culture status in 1990, the city has never looked back. And unlike its more conservative rival to the east, Edinburgh, Glasgow has never been afraid to take risks. After all, this is the city of Charles Rennie Mackintosh, that indisputable genius of architecture and design who was decades ahead of his time. From the ultramodern "Armadillo" (actually the Clyde Auditorium), which recalls the sleek sophistication of the Sydney Opera House, to Mackintosh's own Glasgow School of Art (guided tours are available), Glasgow's city streets are awash with new and old landmarks.

In 1999 Glasgow earned yet another accolade: U.K. City of Architecture and Design. To celebrate its architectural heritage the city welcomed a new addition to the skyline. The Lighthouse, a $19.6 million restoration of the old Glasgow Herald building located in Mitchell Lane off Buchanan Street, opened during the summer of 1999, to much anticipation. The first major building designed by Mackintosh, the revamped structure is reportedly Europe's largest center for design and architecture. It contains an interpretation center on Mackintosh's life and work, permanent exhibits, a 100-seat conference room, and a café.

Other important Mackintosh sites in the city include the Willow Tea Rooms on Sauchiehall Street and Buchanan Street, the Daily Record Building (exterior only), Martyrs School, Queens Cross Church (headquarters of the Mackintosh Society), and Scotland Street School. It's also worth the effort to visit Hill House, in nearby

Helensburgh—a train from Central Station will take you to the town in about 30 minutes, and then there's an additional 1.5 mile hike from the Helensburgh Central station to Hill House. A good investment is the Mackintosh Trail Ticket, which is available at travel centers and online at the Mackintosh Society web site for only £10. It provides unlimited travel on local bus and subway services and includes entry to all participating Mackintosh attractions in and around Glasgow. For more information, contact the Charles Rennie Mackintosh Society at (0141) 946-6600 or visit their web site at www.crmsociety.com.

The most popular attraction in Glasgow remains the always-impressive Burrell Collection, which houses over 8,000 objects under a glass roof in a leafy section of the city. Meanwhile, in the center of town, the Gallery of Modern Art contains four floors devoted to the work of living artists from throughout the world.

The Tenement House is a typical Victorian tenement flat circa 1892. Once the home of an ordinary Glasgow shorthand typist, who lived here for more than 50 years, the house has been turned into a fascinating living history museum of sorts.

If you want to learn more about the lives of ordinary Glaswegians, a visit to the People's Palace in Glasgow Green is essential. The Palace, which celebrated its 100th anniversary in January 1998, contains all kinds of artifacts and mementos connected with the lives of ordinary Glasgow men and women. It's fun, informative, and, best of all, free!

But there's also an older Glasgow to explore as well. Within the Cathedral District on the east side of town, once the center of civil and ecclesiastical government in Glasgow, stands dark and gaunt Glasgow Cathedral. One of the finest examples of Gothic architecture in Scotland, here you will find the tomb of St. Mungo, or Kentigern, Glasgow's patron saint. Also in the district and definitely worth a sustained visit is the St. Mungo Museum of Religious Life and Art, reportedly the only museum of its kind in the world.

Argyll Hotel
973 Sauchiehall Street
Glasgow
Telephone: 0141-337-3313
Fax: 0141-337-3283
E-mail: info@argyllhotelglasgow.co.uk
Web site: www.argyllhotelglasgow.co.uk
Bedrooms: 38 rooms, all ensuite.
Rates: From £36 per person. **Credit cards:** Yes. **Open:** Year-round.
Children: Yes. **Pets:** No. **Smoking:** Yes. **Provision for handicapped:** Yes.
Directions: Located in the city's West End, a 5-minute drive from
Central and Queen Street railway stations. The closest underground is
Kelvinhall, a 5-minute walk away.

Located in the West End, this Georgian building is within walking
distance of the Scottish Exhibition and Conference Centre,
Kelvingrove Art Gallery, Glasgow University, and Kelvingrove Park.
Shoppers note: IKEA is only a 15-minute drive away. The hotel's in-
house restaurant, Sutherlands, has an open fire, dim lighting, and
overall cozy atmosphere. The Argyll also works with various cultural
organizations to sponsor short breaks, such as a city golf break,
Scottish opera break, theatre breaks, historical tours, and Mackintosh
in Style Weekends. The latter features an inclusive weekend package
that includes an illustrated introductory talk at the Argyll on a Friday
evening and continues with 2 days of guided bus tours to the Glasgow
School of Art, the Mackintosh House, Queen's Cross Church, House
for an Art Lover, the Willow Tea Rooms, and Hill House in
Helensburgh.

Babbity Bowster
Fraser Laurie
16-18 Blackfriars Street
Glasgow
Telephone: 0141-552-5055
Fax: 0141-552-7774
Bedrooms: 6 rooms, all ensuite.
Rates: £30 single, £55 double. **Credit cards:** MasterCard/Eurocard, American Express, VISA. **Open:** All year except Christmas Day and New Year's Day. **Children:** All ages. **Pets:** Yes. **Smoking:** Yes. **Provision for handicapped:** No. **Directions:** Located in the Merchant City between George Street and Argyle Street.

With a name like Babbity Bowster, you know you're in for something unusual. Located in the Merchant City, as the fashionable East End of the city is now called, the Bowster is an old building. Designed by noted Scot architect James Adam in 1792, it underwent a major facelift in 1985. It is said to be located on the site of a former monastery and at one point in its past was a coffeehouse frequented by the Tobacco Lords, who made their fortune in the American colonies during pre-Revolutionary days. The unusual name is reportedly taken from a dance called "the babbity bowster," "babbity" meaning "bob at the" and "bowster" meaning large pillow. Today it is a popular combination café, bar, hotel, and restaurant.

The Babbity consists of three levels. The bedrooms are located on the top floor; the Schottische restaurant and dining room is on the second floor, and the pub and café are on the ground level. Meals in the baronial Schottische Restaurant upstairs are served on round and oval wooden tables. In the evening the restaurant adopts a more romantic and sophisticated mood, with candles glowing on each table. Breakfast is served on the ground floor.

The pub has an appropriately worn look, without being shabby, although recently the décor has been upgraded a bit. The food is filling, tasty, and nourishing; the attentive and gregarious young waitstaff are always ready to assist. Spend a few hours here in the evening and you're guaranteed to meet more than a few characters, from visiting musicians (music sessions are popular at the Babbity) to brainy schoolteachers on their way home after a long day in the classroom. Throughout it all, Fraser Laurie, the friendly movie-star-handsome owner with a patch over one eye, watches attentively. A happy observation: there are no televisions on the premises. With so many interesting specimens of humanity coming and going through the front door, how can you not be entertained?

Cathedral House
Mr. B. McAneny
28-32 Cathedral Square
Glasgow
Telephone: 0141-552-3519
Fax: 0141-552-2444
Bedrooms: 6 rooms with bath and shower, 2 rooms with shower.
Rates: £49 single, £69 double. **Credit cards:** VISA, American Express, Diners Club, MasterCard. **Open:** Year-round except Christmas and New Year's Day. **Children:** Yes. **Pets:** Yes. **Smoking:** Yes. **Provision for handicapped:** Only in café bar. **Directions:** From airport follow the M8 to Glasgow City Centre, taking the Glasgow Cathedral exit, which will take you to a set of traffic lights facing the Royal Infirmary. Follow the road to the right and turn left at the next set of lights. Cathedral House is the first building on the right.

Situated in the Cathedral District, in the medieval heart of old Glasgow, the Cathedral House is located just steps away from the thirteenth-century Glasgow Cathedral, the Provand's Lordship (the oldest house in Glasgow), and the Necropolis, a truly grand Victorian cemetery. The hotel itself has a colorful history. It was established in 1877 as a hostel by the Discharged Prisoners Aid Society and built in the Scottish baronial style. Restored in 1990, the hotel to this day remains faithful to the original design. There is an excellent upstairs restaurant that is unusual in another way—it is the only Icelandic restaurant in Glasgow, indeed perhaps in all of Scotland. Among its specialties include Scottish game, poultry, and fish. The meat and fish courses are cooked Icelandic style at the table. Local jazz, folk, and blues acts are regularly featured. All in all, Cathedral House is a friendly, down-to-earth historic gem.

Kirklee Hotel
Douglas and Rosemary Rogen
11 Kensington Gate
Glasgow
Telephone: 0141-334-5555
Fax: 0141-339-3828
E-mail: kirklee@clara.net
Web site: www.kirkleehotel.co.uk
Bedrooms: 9 rooms, all ensuite.
Rates: £72 double. Credit cards: VISA, MasterCard. **Open:** Year-round
except Christmas Eve and Christmas Day. **Children:** Yes. **Pets:** No.
Smoking: No. **Provision for handicapped:** No. **Directions:** Take the
Great Western Road (A82) to Horselethill Road. Kensington Gate is
the first on the right.

Set in Glasgow's West End, this gracious Edwardian lodging is full
of character and forms a part of Kensington Gate, a series of red sandstone townhouses. The Kirklee is situated away from the main roads
and overlooks a private park, so a restful night is assured. The terrace
was designed by David Barclay in 1902 and built in the grand style of
the townhouses of the era. You enter through a grand door and into
a paneled hallway. Period furniture and oil paintings by Scottish and
international artists add to the old-world atmosphere, as do the gold
and deep blue colors, carved fireplace, and original parquet floors.
Tall oriole windows overlook the private gardens. All rooms are individually furnished with lovely fabrics and designs. Unlike most establishments, breakfast is served in your room. The Rogens are a helpful
couple who do their best to make you feel at home. The Kirklee is a
short walk from the many restaurants and bars along busy Byres Road,
the West End's major thoroughfare. Opulent, dignified, and
supremely civilized, the Kirklee is a delight any way you look at it.

The Manor Park Hotel
Catherine and Angus
28 Balshagray Drive
Glasgow
Telephone: 0141-339-2143
Fax: 0141-339-5842
Bedrooms: 10, all ensuite.
Rates: £35-50 single, £50-65 double. **Credit cards:** American Express, Diners Club, MasterCard, VISA, Switch. **Open:** Year-round. **Children:** Yes. **Pets:** By arrangement. **Smoking:** No. **Provision for handicapped:** Disabled access ground floor bedroom only. **Directions:** Located in the West End, opposite Victoria Park.

The Manor Park Hotel qualifies as one of Glasgow's most unusual hotels by virtue of its staff—it reportedly is the only Gaelic hotel in town. That's right. Everyone here speaks Gaelic (as well as English, of course). The innkeeper, Angus, is a native Gaelic speaker who hails from the island of Eriskay. Even the rooms have Gaelic names such as Hiort for St. Kilda or Na Hearadh for Harris. Located in the West End, this restored Victorian town house is close to all the cultural activities, fine restaurants, and pubs.

Nairns
Nick and Topher Nairns
13 Woodside Crescent
Glasgow
Telephone: 0141-353-0707
Fax: 0141-331-1684
E-mail: info@nairns.co.uk
Web site: www.nairns.co.uk
Bedrooms: 4 rooms, all ensuite.
Rates: From £90 to £125 per room. **Credit cards:** MasterCard/
Eurocard, American Express, VISA, Diners Club, Switch, Delta. **Open:**
Year-round except Christmas, Boxing Day (December 26), New Year's
Day, and January 2. **Children:** No. **Pets:** No. **Provision for handi-
capped:** No. **Directions:** From Charing Cross turn into Woodlands
Road, then take the first road on the left, Lynedoch Street, and then
make another left onto Lynedoch Terrace and still another left onto
Woodside Terrace. Woodside Crescent, located just off Sauchiehall
Street, is a continuation of Woodside Terrace.

Nairns is a converted townhouse located on a quiet Georgian crescent and only a 10-minute walk from Glasgow City center. It is perhaps
better known for its restaurant and its celebrity chef, Nick Nairns, who
is one of Scotland's most highly respected and deservedly popular
restaurateurs. Essentially Nairns is a five-star restaurant with rooms.
The restaurant takes up two floors. The formal dining room upstairs
serves sophisticated and innovative food to national and international
acclaim. (All of this luxury comes at a cost, of course). The downstairs eatery is more casual, with its modern dark benches and cool
grayish walls.

As expected, the accommodations are just as ritzy. The Silver Room
exudes, as its name indicates, a cool reserve, with steel bedposts. It's

oh-so modern and minimalist. If Philip Glass were to design a hotel room, one imagines it would look like this. On the other side of the spectrum is the Amber Room, which projects a warm reddish glow. The Nantucket Room is done up in soft muted pale green; the striking bathroom, complete with red floor and red ceiling, includes a claw-footed tub. The "painterly" Vermeer Room features a trompe l'oeil effect. Sienna-colored doorways lead to the illusion of a balcony. Continental breakfast is extra at £7.50. A two-course lunch costs £13.50; a three-course, £17.

The Pipers' Tryst Hotel
Gemma Laidlaw, general manager
30-34 McPhater Street
Cowcaddens
Glasgow
Telephone: 0141-353-5551
Fax: 0141-353-1570
E-mail: hotel@thepipingcentre.co.uk
Web site: www.thepipingcentre.co.uk
Bedrooms: 8 rooms, all ensuite.
Rates: £50 single, £65 double (special rates for students attending the piping school are available upon request). **Credit cards:** VISA.
Open: Year-round. **Children:** Yes. **Pets:** No. **Smoking:** Yes. **Provision for handicapped:** No. **Directions:** Located a short walk north of Sauchiehall Street, Glasgow's commercial center.

Built in 1873 and located in the theater district, the building has been spruced up and the interior thoroughly modernized. The Piper's Tryst opened in May 1996 as a combination bed and breakfast, café, and museum. The 8 rooms are comfortable and modern, without being too sterile. Extras include a trouser press and hair dryers. Complimentary continental breakfast can be served in your room at your request. If you wish to have a full Scottish breakfast, which includes generous helpings of bacon, fried eggs, tomatoes, sautéed potatoes, mushrooms, black pudding, potato scones, sausages, tea or coffee, and hot buttered toast for £3.50, make your way to the café. Downstairs is the National Museum of Piping, with its exhibits on the piping tradition, the music of the bagpipes, and the history of important piping families, including the most famous of all, the

MacCrimmons of Skye. Among the items on display are various sets of pipes, from the Highland war pipes to the lesser-known Scottish small pipes. The center also contains a school with rehearsal rooms, a performance hall, reference library, conference facilities, and gift shop. Anyone who loves the pipes must stay here.

ALSO RECOMMENDED

Glasgow, *Adelaide's Guest House,* 209 Bath Street. Telephone: 0141-248-4970. Fax: 0141-226-4247. info@adelaides.freeserve.co.uk. 8 rooms, most ensuite. Adelaide serves many functions. It's a guest house set in a 19th-century building, but also a Baptist church and a pre-school nursery for children ages 6 weeks to 5 years. It also has a multi-purpose auditorium that can seat 450 and a small meeting room for up to 15 people. All rooms are non-smoking. Families and children are particularly welcome. Singles range from £25-32, doubles are £35. All prices though are room only. Breakfast costs £2 for a light breakfast, £3.50 for a continental breakfast, and £6 for a traditional Scottish breakfast.

Glasgow, *Albion Hotel,* 405-407 North Woodside Road. Telephone: 0141-339-8620. Fax: 0141-334-8159. 20 rooms, all ensuite. Located across from Kelvinbridge tube station in the heart of the West End.

Glasgow, *Amadeus Guesthouse,* 411 North Woodside Road. Vivienne Ennemoser. Telephone: 0141-339-8257. Privately run B&B in a Victorian townhouse in the West End. The proprietor is a Mozart aficionado. Her continental-style breakfast of ham and cheese, cereals, yogurt, fruit, rolls, fruit juice, coffee or tea is accompanied by the music of the celebrated musician as well as Brahms and Schubert. Rooms in the front overlook the River Kelvin. Singles range from £20-27, doubles £40-48. Non-smoking throughout. Most rooms are ensuite.

Glasgow, *Angus Hotel,* 970 Sauchiehall Street. Telephone: 0141-357-5155. Fax: 0141-339-9469. E-mail: info@angushotelglasgow.co.uk. Website:www.angushotelglasgow.co.uk. 18 rooms, all ensuite. Charming Georgian townhouse in a great part of town at affordable rates (around £44 single, £58 double). Sister hotel to the Argyll Hotel (see separate listing).

Glasgow, *Arthouse Hotel,* 129 Bath Street. Telephone: 0141-221-6789. Web site: www.arthousehotel.com. 65 rooms, all ensuite. Stylish, bold, and cheeky—that in a nutshell is the Arthouse Hotel. Located in the city center, the historic structure was built in 1911 and restored in 1999. Although rates are based on a room-only basis (doubles start from £115), weekend stays do include breakfast. The Arthouse Grill is a popular night spot. Very friendly staff.

Glasgow, *Atlantic Guest House Hotel,* 232 Renfrew Street. Telephone: 0141-332-0000. Fax: 0141-333-0100. E-mail: info@atlantic-hotel.biz.

14 rooms, all ensuite. The folks here specialize in budget accommodation: singles at £29 per person, doubles from £22-26.

Glasgow, *Groucho Saint Jude's,* 190 Bath Street. Telephone: 0141-352-8800. Fax: 0141-352-8801. E-mail: info@saintjudes.com. 6 rooms, all ensuite. Small, stylish boutique hotel in the city center. Features an excellent restaurant on the ground floor that specializes in contemporary cuisine and a trendy bar in the basement.

Glasgow, *Hillview Guest House,* 18 Hillhead Street. Telephone: 0141-334-5585. Fax: 0141-353-3155. 10 rooms. Small and friendly West End guesthouse near the university and the Botanic Gardens.

Glasgow, *Inn on the Green,* 25 Greenhead Street. Telephone: 0141-554-0165. Fax: 0141-556-4678. E-mail: sales@theinnonthegreen.co.uk. Web site: www.theinnonthegreen.co.uk. 18 rooms, all ensuite. Both a hotel and a restaurant, the Inn on the Green lives up to its name. It is located on the edge of Glasgow Green on the city's East Side. Singles start at £55, doubles from £75. All rooms are non-smoking. Live jazz and pre-theatre dinner menu, too.

Glasgow, *Kirkland House,* 42 St. Vincent Crescent. Telephone: 0141-248-3458. Fax: 0141-221-5174. E-mail: kirkland@gisp.net. 6 rooms, 3 ensuite. Family-owned guesthouse in the West End. Reasonable and neat. Great for all West End attractions.

Glasgow, *The Merchant Lodge* (formerly the Courtyard Hotel), 52 Virginia Street. Telephone: 0141-552-2424. Fax: 0141-552-4747. 34 rooms, all ensuite. Great value in the city center. This Merchant City accommodation is located in one of Glasgow's oldest buildings. Includes a cobblestoned courtyard and an old turnpike stair, one of the last in Glasgow still in use. Originally home to the city's Tobacco Lords. Near George Square, the City Chambers, Queen Street, and Central stations. Handsomely modern interior too: hardwood floors, pine furniture, and wicker chairs.

Glasgow, *Number Thirty-Six,* 36 St. Vincent Crescent. John and Julie MacKay. Telephone: 0141-248-2086. Fax: 0141-221-1477. E-mail: no36@no36.co.uk. 6 rooms, all ensuite or with private facilities. Friendly, family-owned Victorian terrace home in the City Center for only £35-40 single, £27.50-32.50 double. Each room is individually designed and furnished in natural woods and fabrics. A continental breakfast is served in your room. No smoking.

Glasgow, *The Old Schoolhouse,* 194 Renfrew Street. Telephone:

0141-332-7600. Fax: 0141-332-8684. E-mail: oschool@hotmail.com. 17 rooms, all ensuite. Nothing particularly fancy here, but you can't beat the price (£28) and convenience (the shops of Sauchiehall Street are a short walk away, and it's down the street from the Glasgow School of Art). All rooms have direct dial telephone, color television, polished pine floors, and matching furniture.

Glasgow, *Park House,* Mrs. D. Hallam, 13 Victoria Park Gardens South. Telephone: 0141-339-1559. Fax: 0141-576-0915. E-mail: xwf54@dial.pipex.com. 3 rooms, 2 ensuite. Handsome Victorian townhouse just 15 minutes from Glasgow Airport and 10 minutes from the city center.

Glasgow, *Rennie Mackintosh Hotel,* 218-220 Renfrew Street. Telephone: 0141-333-9992. Fax: 0141-333-9995. 42 rooms, all ensuite. Mackintosh-themed B&B a short walk from Mackintosh's masterpiece, the Glasgow School of Art. Rates here are £32.95 single; £52.95 double.

Glasgow, *Scott's Guest House,* Kay and Bob Scott, 417 North Woodside Road. Telephone: 0141-339-3750. 8 rooms, all ensuite. This quiet guesthouse, just off busy Great Western Road in Glasgow's leafy West End, overlooks Kelvin Park. Peaceful.

Glasgow, *Smith's Hotel,* 963 Sauchiehall Street. Telephone: 0141-339-7674. Fax: 0141-334-1892. E-mail: info@smiths-hotel.com. Web site: www.smiths-hotel.com. 7 rooms, most ensuite. Established in 1928, this family run hotel is located in the West End. Reliable and affordable. Singles range from £21-36, doubles average £26 per person.

Glasgow, *The Town House,* 4 Hughenden Terrace. Telephone: 0141-357-0862. Fax: 0141-339-9605. E-mail: hospitality@thetownhouseglasgow.com. Web site: www.thetownhouseglasgow.com. 10 rooms, all ensuite. The Town House forms part of a tree-lined terrace of renovated Victorian townhouses.

Glasgow, *The Townhouse Hotel,* 21 Royal Crescent. Telephone: 0141-332-9009. 19 rooms, all ensuite. Singles in this West End establishment are £30, doubles £55.

Inverary, *Creagh Dhubh,* Richard and Janice MacLugash. Telephone: 01499-302430. E-mail: stay@creagdhubh.com, Web site: www.creagdhubh.com. 5 rooms, all ensuite. Handsome stone-built guesthouse with large garden located on the edge of town. Spacious rooms; some come with a loch view.

Central & Tayside

The focal point of the Scottish heartland converges in the old town of Stirling, once the Scottish capital and still a formidable place steeped in history and rife with atmospherics. Indeed, it has often been called Edinburgh in miniature.

The highlight of any visit to Stirling is a stop by Stirling Castle, that impenetrable fortress that looms high over the town, pondering the town's past and present like some watchful sentinel. From the castle, take the time to admire the buildings of Stirling's Old Town. Nearby is the National Wallace Monument, an angular and distinctive landmark that can be seen from miles around.

A short distance from Stirling is the beauty of the Trossachs, that lush wooded paradise that has been attracting visitors since Sir Walter Scott first wrote about the area in the early nineteenth century. Among the many handsome towns and villages in the area include Callander, Aberfoyle, and Strathyre. The Rob Roy and Trossachs Visitor Centre in Callander is a good place to receive an introduction to the area, and a little bit about the legend and life of Rob Roy MacGregor, the Scottish folk hero whose colorful life was portrayed by Liam Neeson in the popular film *Rob Roy*.

The commercial heart of the area called Perthshire in the Tayside region is the handsome city of Perth. Three things helped to bring prosperity to Perth: salmon, wool, and whisky. And to that we might add tourism, for the visitor trade is placed quite high on the list of economic forces. Although Perth gained its royal burgh status in 1210, not much of old Perth remains. It looks very much a twentieth-century city, with the requisite upscale malls and shopping and substantial homes. But Perth also has its artistic side, being the home of the imposing Perth Museum and Art Gallery and the Perth Theatre.

The best-known theater festival in the region must belong to the Pitlochry Festival Theatre. Housed in a modern building that Prince Charles officially dedicated on July 9, 1981, the theater is located on the south bank of the River Tummel with views of Ben y Vrackie beyond.

One of the most charming villages around is Dunkeld, once the ecclesiastical capital of Scotland. For such a small place, it has much to see. A short walk along Cathedral Street leads to the cathedral itself, a mixture of Gothic and Norman styles, which sits serenely on the banks of the River Tay. The cathedral is dedicated to St. Columba. According to tradition, his relics were buried under the chancel steps. Construction on the cathedral began in 1318, but the lovely structure was reduced to ruin during the Reformation. The choir, re-roofed in 1660, now serves as the parish church and is open daily. You will find a small museum in the fifteenth-century sacristy, which can be entered through the choir. The ruined fifteenth-century nave and tower are entrusted to the care of Historic Scotland.

Both Dunkeld and the adjacent Victorian village of Birnam are within walking distance of each other. Located in the center of Birnam is the Beatrix Potter Garden, which at first glance may seem an unusual place for a memorial to the creator of Peter Rabbit and other endearing childhood characters. Actually Potter had spent her childhood holidays here and drew inspiration from the area and its people for her Peter Rabbit tales.

Antique lovers need look no further than the indoor Scottish Antique & Arts Centre, near the tiny Perthshire village of Abernyte. Thirty dealers offer their antiques, art, rugs, pottery, furniture, and other wares. The centre is open seven days a week, from 10 A.M. to 5 P.M. There's also a lovely café on the premises.

Monachyle Mhor
Tom Lewis
Balquhidder
Lochearnhead
Perthshire
Telephone: 01877-384622
Fax: 01877-384305
E-mail: info@monachylemhor.com
Web site: www.monachylemhor.com
Bedrooms: 11 rooms, all ensuite.
Rates: £95-220 double. **Credit cards:** VISA, Access, Switch, MasterCard.
Open: February-December. **Children:** 12 and older. **Pets:** No. **Smoking:**
In bar only. **Provision for handicapped:** Bar and restaurant only.
Directions: 11 miles north of Callander on A84. Turn right at Kinghouse
Hotel and carry on up the glen road about four miles to Balquhidder.

Situated on their own 2,000 acres of land, the Lewis family runs
both the farming enterprise and the hotel that offers modern comfort
with the best of country living. One of the sons, Dick, runs the farm
and is the head shepherd; the older son, Tom, is head chef.
Monachyle Mhor was reportedly the first home of Rob Roy
MacGregor, when the outlaw married at the age of twenty-one. Now
it is a lovely small farmhouse hotel located at the end of a long and
winding road (and since it is Scotland, of course, it is also a narrow
one). The highly acclaimed restaurant on the premises is known for its
game and herbs taken from the estate. Most of the produce comes
from a 30-mile radius. The estate itself has magnificent views of Loch
Voil and Loch Doine. The handsome dining room sports salmon-col-
ored walls and oaken tables and chairs, along with old prints of black-
face sheep and cattle. The bedrooms are especially attractive, tastefully
and imaginatively decorated. The Lewises offer private salmon and
trout fishing, with red deer stalking and grouse shooting in season.

Arden House
Ian M. Mitchell and William R. Jackson
Bracklinn Road
Callander
Perthshire
Telephone/Fax: 01877-330235
Web site: www.ardenhouse.org.uk
E-mail: ardenhouse@onetel.com
Bedrooms: 6 rooms, all ensuite.
Rates: Easter to late October £32.50-35 single, £60-72 double/twin.
Credit cards: VISA, MasterCard. **Open:** April to late October.
Children: Children over 13. **Pets:** No. **Smoking:** No. **Provision for handicapped:** 2 ground floor rooms. 5 steps up to front door.
Directions: If traveling north by car, leave the M9 motorway at Junction 10 north of Stirling, signposted to Crianlarich. Follow the A84 to Callander. In Callander turn right into Bracklinn Road before entering the village center. Arden House is 200 yards on the left.

Arden House stands in its own garden overlooking the attractive village of Callander, with wonderful views of nearby Ben Ledi and surrounding countryside. It's only a few minutes' walk from the village center. The house itself is a large Victorian stone-built dwelling with greenery on one side and woods at the rear. Two of the bedrooms are on the ground floor, as is the comfy sitting room. Callander, often called the gateway to the Trossachs, served as the model for the fictional Tannochbrae, made famous (throughout Britain at least) by the popular BBC television series *Dr. Finlay's Casebook*. Arden House was the television home of Drs. Finlay and Cameron and their housekeeper, Janet. In addition to being only a two-minute walk from Callander's 18-hole golf course, Arden House is also close enough to enjoy the various summer cruises on Loch Lomond and Loch Katrine. Your hosts Ian and William not only "guarantee you a warm welcome to our home," the dynamic duo also serve fabulous full Scottish breakfasts.

The Pend
Peter and Marina Braney
5 Brae Street
Dunkeld
Telephone: 01350-727586
Fax: 01350-727173
E-mail: molly@thepend.sol.co.uk
Web site: www.thepend.com
Bedrooms: 6 rooms, with private facilities.
Rates: £35 pp., £60 pp. (includes dinner.) **Credit cards:** VISA, MasterCard, Eurocheque, Delta, JCB, American Express, Diners Club, Switch. **Children:** Yes; no charge for children up to 3 years. Children from 3 to 11 get half off. **Pets:** Yes. **Smoking:** In bedrooms and lounge only. **Provision for handicapped:** No. **Directions:** Located a short walk or drive up from Dunkeld Cathedral, just off Atholl Road, Dunkeld's commercial street.

Situated up a hill off the main street of town and a short walk from Dunkeld Cathedral, the Pend sports a deceptively unassuming Georgian facade from the outside. But step inside and you'll be pleasantly surprised, for here you'll find six elegantly spacious rooms as well as a warm and friendly greeting from Peter and Marina (English and Irish, respectively) and their frisky Westie named Molly. Formerly a family home, the Braneys bought the property in 1997. "Our guests always come first," they say, and it shows. The rooms are furnished with many fine antiques. Each room comes equipped with a hand basin, luxury bathrobe, and color television. Although there are no ensuite facilities as of this writing, two large bathrooms are provided for the use of guests.

Meals are served in the splendid sitting/dining room, beautifully decorated with its mustard walls and antique furniture. The four-course meal is something to behold and one that reflects the variety of fish, meat, game, fruit, vegetables, and cheeses of Perthshire. Breakfast is served when you want it—in other words, at the Pend you can sleep in without feeling guilty or pressured. Breakfast consists of a light selection (cereals, croissants, breads, fresh and preserved fruits) or a traditional Scottish breakfast but with a twist—scrambled eggs with local smoked salmon, Arbroath smokies (smoked haddock), porridge, and even haggis. Dietary needs can be accommodated as well.

Guests of the Pend can use the leisure club facilities of the nearby Stakis Dunkeld House Hotel at discounted rates. Facilities include a heated indoor swimming pool, spa bath, sauna, steam room, multipurpose gymnasium, tennis, croquet, putting, and archery. Also available are massage, beauty treatments, and a tanning salon. Enjoy the lovely walks along the River Tay and through the almost 200 acres of hotel grounds, which include a shooting range, salmon fishing, and mountain-bike rental. The Braneys are truly gracious people, and in the Pend you will enjoy one of the finest B&B experiences in all of Scotland. Tip: if possible, request the room at the top. It's quite a view.

Inverbeg Inn
Adrian D. Hanger
Inverbeg
Near Luss
Telephone: 01436-860678
Fax: 01436-860686
E-mail: inverbeg@onyxnet.co.uk; info@inverbeg.co.uk
Web site: www.scottish-selection.co.uk
Bedrooms: 20 rooms, all ensuite.
Rates: £75-85 single, L115-140 double double. **Credit cards:** VISA,
American Express, MasterCard, Switch, Solo. **Open:** All year. **Children:**
Yes. **Pets:** No. **Smoking:** No. **Provision for handicapped:** Yes.
Directions: 3 miles north of Luss on the main route to the West Coast
and the Mull of Kintyre. From Glasgow follow the signs for the Erskine
bridge and then on to Loch Lomond along the A82.

One of the best-known small hotels in Scotland, the Inverbeg Inn is
situated on the bonny banks of Loch Lomond, just beyond the tiny village of Luss. You couldn't ask for a better location. It's an area where
truly breathtaking scenery, history, and culture come together. And if
for some reason, and it's hard to imagine how, you ever tire of the
many rural attractions, be assured that the thrills of big-city life—in
this case, Glasgow—are only a short half-hour away. The inn itself
dates back to 1814. The lodge on the loch side looks east to Ben
Lomond and Ben Vrakie. Each spacious room has its own individual
character. With their warm yellow-tinged walls, the overall effect is of
genuine good will. The inn specializes in local produce, including
such tasty items as Loch Fyne oysters, scallops, salmon, Angus beef,
Glen Finnart venison, and even herbs from the garden. Owner Adrian
D. Hanger always makes sure that an excellent range of single malt
whiskies is always in stock.

The Lomond Country Inn
David Adams
Kinnesswood
By Loch Leven
Telephone: 01592-840253
Fax: 01592-840693
E-mail: the.lomond@dial.pipex.com
Web site: www.smoothhound.co.uk/
Bedrooms: 12 rooms, all ensuite.
Rates: £45-50 single, £32.50-35 double. **Credit cards:** MasterCard/
Eurocard, American Express, VISA, Diners Club, Switch, Delta.
Open: Year-round. **Pets:** Yes. **Smoking:** Restricted. **Provision for
handicapped:** Yes. **Directions:** Get off at Junction 5 on the M90 and
follow signs for Scotlandwell. The Lomond Country Inn is located
in the next village.

This friendly, reasonably priced, and cozy family-run hotel offers
magnificent views over Loch Leven in the village of Kinnesswood.
Of the 12 rooms, four are located in the inn itself and the other
eight are in a modern extension opposite. The Lomond Country
Inn is within an hour's drive of 50-plus golf courses, as well as ample
riding, walking, rambling, and birdwatching opportunities. In other
words, this is peak outdoor country. If all this weren't enough, there
are close to a dozen stillwater fisheries and four nearby rivers
stocked with brown trout, rainbow trout, salmon, and sea trout.
Cycling and walking paths are within close proximity, and in the
summer there is a boat crossing to Loch Leven Castle, once the
prison home of Mary, Queen of Scots, for over a year. The inn specializes in fresh seafood and freshwater fish, game, beef, lamb, vegetables, and seasonal fruit. The cost for a three-course dinner
ranges from an affordable £10 to £14.

Craigroyston House
Douglas and Gretta Maxwell
2 Lower Oakfield
Pitlochry
Telephone/Fax: 01796-472053
E-mail: reservations@craigroyston.co.uk
Web site: www.craigroyston.co.uk
Bedrooms: 8 rooms, all ensuite.
Rates: £25-32 per person. **Credit cards:** No. **Open:** Year-round except Christmas. **Children:** No. **Pets:** No. **Smoking:** No. **Provision for handicapped:** No. **Directions:** From Atholl Road, Pitlochry's main street, go past Bonnet Hill Road to East Moulin Road. From East Moulin Road turn onto Lower Oakfield Road.

Douglas Maxwell is a definite charmer, a natural salesman (and that is meant in the best sense of the word) who makes everyone who walks through his door feel at ease. He and his wife, Gretta, run their guesthouse with gentle efficiency. Craigroyston is a short walk from the railway station, set in its own ground, and is located just off Pitlochry's main road. The bedrooms are spacious and elegant in an old-fashioned way. The cozy lounge boasts a log fire. Among the added touches that the Maxwells offer are drying, ironing, and shoe-cleaning services. Outside Craigroyston's front door lies Pitlochry itself. Pitlochry started out as a tiny hamlet back in 1727. Now it's one of the most popular resort towns in Scotland. Take the time to walk along the main street, have a cup of tea and a sweet in its tearooms, or simply window-shop at its many marvelous gift and woolen stores.

Ferryman's Cottage
Kath Sanderson
Port-Na-Craig
Pitlochry
Telephone: 01796-473681
E-mail: info@ferrymanscottage.co.uk
Web site: www.ferrymanscottage.co.uk
Bedrooms: 2 rooms, both ensuite.
Rates: £25-30 pp. **Credit cards:** No. **Open:** Closed Christmas and New Year's. **Children:** 12 and older. **Pets:** No. **Provision for handicapped:** No. **Directions:** Two minutes from the A9, Ferryman's Cottage is situated below the Festival Theatre, the Dam and Fish Ladder, and by the suspension bridge below the theater.

The tiny historic hamlet of Port-Na-Craig was established about 300 years ago. The cottage functioned as the boat house before the bridge over the River Tummel was built to serve the resident population and cattle crossing the river. The cottage looks almost doll-like, sitting as it does by the river's edge. A riot of flowers adds color to the picture-postcard scene. Inside you'll find cozy and oh-so-comfy rooms, one ensuite, but all with color television and tea- and coffee-making facilities. A full Scottish breakfast is served in the compact dining room, which overlooks the River Tummel, renowned for its salmon. Port-Na-Craig is a short walk across the suspension bridge to Pitlochry. There is also a lovely garden and stone patio. The cottage is immediately adjacent to the Wee Kiosk ice cream stand, a temptation for those with a sweet tooth, especially during the height of summer.

Portnacraig Inn & Restaurant
Bill and Andrew Bryan
Portnacraig
Pitlochry
Telephone: 01796-472777
Bedrooms: 2 rooms, both ensuite.
Rates: £25 pp. ensuite. **Credit cards:** MasterCard/Eurocard, VISA,
Switch, Delta. **Open:** Year-round. **Children:** Yes. **Pets:** Yes (well
behaved). **Smoking:** Yes. **Provision for handicapped:** No. **Directions:**
Located just over the suspension bridge in the tiny hamlet of Port-
Na-Craig.

This lovely old stone inn on the banks of the River Tummel dates
from circa 1650. It's located directly below the Pitlochry Festival
Theatre. Although more of a restaurant than a bona fide inn—it only
has two rooms after all—it's such an utterly charming place that I had
to include it. The tiny windows of the bistro-style restaurant also overlook the river. The service is extremely friendly and very casual. If
you're planning to attend a show at the festival theatre across the road
you can dine alfresco (weather permitting of course) on the patio.
And if the weather doesn't cooperate (this is Scotland), then you can
take great pleasure in appreciating some of the nice touches found
within the interior: low-beamed ceiling, green tablecloths, printed cur-
tains, mauve-colored walls, and dark wooden chairs. The restaurant is
open daily from 10 A.M.

Creagan House
Gordon and Cherry Gunn
Strathyre
Near Callander
Telephone: 01877-384638
Fax: 01877-384319
E-mail: eatandstay@creaganhouse.co.uk
Bedrooms: 5 rooms, all ensuite.
Rates: £57.50 single, £47.50 pp. double. **Credit cards:** MasterCard,
American Express, VISA. **Open:** March to January. **Children:** Yes (chil-
dren's tea served at 6 P.M. but no one under 10 for dinner). **Pets:** Yes.
Smoking: In lounge only. **Provision for handicapped:** On ground-floor
bedroom only. **Directions:** Located along the A84, about .25 mile
north of Strathyre.

The Gunns do their best to retain the simple charm of their seventeenth-century farmhouse. The location couldn't be better—a peaceful spot surrounded by lovely scenery. The tiny and charming village
of Strathrye is located at the head of Loch Lubnaig. Nearby are major
historical sites (Rob Roy's grave, Stirling Castle), yet Creagan House
seems far away from the rest of the world. Gordon and Cherry offer
five charming rooms (one with a fourposter bed) and many thoughtful extras thrown in. The Gunns bought Creagan in 1986, and they
run the B&B with their daughter Maria. Gordon has won accolades for
his cooking—variations on classical French cooking with Scottish
influences. They use fresh produce, much of it grown for them in
organic small holdings.

Dinner is served amid the splendor of the baronial dining hall. Two
menus are offered: the menu of the day for £18.50 and the "Chef's

Favourite" at £22.50. A typical dinner may consist of a warm plate of scallops, lobster, and crab with scallop roe sauce, or roast tomato and basil oil, followed by a choice of poached turbot on tarragon vegetables or spinach and pine nut-crusted rack of lamb with pear purée in a minted pea sauce or filet of venison with glazed sweet potato. For dessert, try the lemon and lime tart with passionfruit coulis, chocolate hazelnut mousse cake, or apple flapjack steamed pudding.

Fairfield Guest House
Mary Hunter
14 Princes Street
Stirling
Telephone: 01786-472685
Bedrooms: 6 rooms, all ensuite.
Rates: From £21. **Credit cards:** None. **Open:** March through October.
Children: All ages. **Pets:** By arrangement. **Smoking:** No. **Provision for handicapped:** No. **Directions:** From the Burghmuir roundabout at the entrance to Stirling, take the second left, passing the bus/railway station. At the roundabout at the railway station turn left into Station Road and then again at the first right at the mini-roundabout at the top of the road. Princes Street is the second left.

This long-established, family-run, and very tidy guesthouse boasts a wonderful location, located as it is just off the town center in a quiet residential cul-de-sac. Stirling Castle is but a short walk away, as are the other sites of the Old Town, including the Old Town Jail, the fifteenth-century Church of the Holy Rude, and Argyll's Lodging, once the residence of the earls, later dukes, of Argyll. Of course, there's plenty of opportunity within walking distance of fine shops and dining. As for the house itself, owner Mary Hunter runs a tight ship. Although only 100 years old (young by Scottish standards!), Fairfield is definitely full of character and period features, which is not to say that modern conveniences are given short shrift. On the contrary, everything appears appropriately contemporary and comfortably furnished. The exterior too is quite welcoming—a warm and mellow honey-colored two-story with a white door.

Kilronan House
Colin and Linda George
15 Kenilworth Road
Bridge of Allan
By Stirling
Telephone: 01786-831054
Web site: www.kilronan.co.uk
Bedrooms: 2, both ensuite.
Rates: £30-35 single, £22-25 double. **Credit cards:** No. **Open:** Year-round. **Children:** Yes. **Pets:** No. **Smoking:** No. **Provision for handicapped:** No. **Directions:** Located on the old A9 road approximately 2 miles north of Stirling. The Bridge of Allan rail station is nearby.

Although only a short distance from the bustling University of Stirling, Kilronan House is located in the quiet village of Bridge of Allan. For its small size, Bridge of Allan has quite a literary history. In 1787 Robert Burns passed through the village—at that time little more than a mill and several cottages, really—en route to the Highland town of Crieff. Burns lingered here long enough to write a poem, "By Allan Stream." During the Victorian era, Bridge of Allan became a popular resort and spa. Many grand houses, such as Kilronan House, which dates back to 1853, were built at that time. For many summers, Robert Louis Stevenson came here on holiday. There is a lovely walk along the river on the old drove road to Dunblane that Stevenson reportedly took. Nearby attractions include Stirling Castle, the Wallace Monument, Bannockburn Visitor Centre and Battlefield, and Loch Katrine.

Tormaukin Country Inn and Restaurant
Alex Simpson
Glendevon
Near Gleneagles
Perthshire
Telephone: 01259-781252
Fax: 01259-781526
E-mail: enquiries@tormaukin.co.uk
Web site: www.tormaukin.co.uk
Bedrooms: 12, all ensuite.
Rates: £60 single, £90 double. **Credit cards:** All major credit cards, including American Express. **Open:** Year-round except Christmas Day and one week in January. **Children:** Yes. **Pets:** With prior arrangement. **Smoking:** Restaurant, non-smoking. Non-smoking bedrooms available. **Provision for handicapped:** No. **Directions:** Located on the old A9 road approximately 2 miles north of Stirling. The Bridge of Allan rail station is nearby.

The Tormaukin was originally an eighteenth-century drovers' inn. Now it is a sympathetically refurbished country inn and restaurant along with self-catering chalet and self-catering bungalow. Off the main road, it is located in a secluded part of Perthshire and yet near many attractions, including distilleries, castles and palaces (Glamis Castle, Blair Castle, and Scone Palace are in the area), and, for golfers, famous Gleneagles. The bedrooms are cozy and rustic and come with such modern conveniences as telephones and satellite TV. Each room is individually decorated. Throughout the year, the Tormaukin offers special packages, such as seasonal breaks, golfing breaks, trout fishing and game- and clay-shooting breaks, and romantic breaks. Don't forget to have a meal in the Tormaukin's excellent restaurant. Very friendly staff too.

ALSO RECOMMENDED

Aberfoyle, *Inchrie Castle—The Covenanters Inn,* Telephone: 01877-382347. Fax: 01877-382785. E-mail: enquiries@inchriecastle.co.uk. 5 single, 18 double, 24 twin, 5 family; all ensuite. Handsome country inn set on a wooded knoll overlooking the village. The inn is graced with singular details—oak beams, log fires, snug lounges—that add to its rustic appeal. Live entertainment is offered on several evenings each week throughout the year.

Aberfoyle, *Creag-Ard House,* Cara Wilson, Milton. Telephone: 01877-382297. 6 rooms, all ensuite. E-mail: cara@creag-ardhouse.co.uk. www.creag-ardhouse.co.uk. Lovely Victorian house nestled in three acres of gardens overlooking Loch Ard, with views to Ben Lomond beyond. Trout fishing and boating rentals can be arranged.

Aberfoyle, *The Forth Inn,* Phil and Tristan Crowder, Main Street. Telephone: 01877-382372. Fax: 01877-382488. E-mail: phil@forthinn.com. 6 rooms, all ensuite. The Forth Inn is located on the main street of Aberfoyle, a pleasant holiday village with plenty of amenities—shops, museums, and outdoor activities, to name but a few—and loads of local character.

Birnam, *Waterbury Guesthouse,* Jane and David Murrell. Telephone: 01350-727324. Fax: 01350-727023. E-mail: info@waterbury-guesthouse.co.uk. Web site: www.waterbury-guesthouse.co.uk. 7 rooms, 6 ensuite. This simple and clean Victorian guesthouse is located in the center of town, across the street from the Beatrix Potter Gardens.

Callander, *Bridgend Cottage,* Diana Hopper, Kilmahog. Telephone: 01877-330385. 3 rooms, all ensuite. Stone-built gamekeepers' cottage located by the riverside. Friendly, relaxed atmosphere. Great area for walking, cycling, and other outdoor activities.

Callander, *Riverview House,* Leny Road. Telephone: 01877-330635. 5 rooms, all ensuite. Victorian house set in its own grounds, within walking distance of shops and attractions.

Killearn, *Black Bull Hotel,* 2 The Square. Telephone: 01360-550215. Fax: 01360-550143. E-mail: blbulluk@aol.com. 10 rooms, all ensuite. Beautifully appointed nineteenth-century hotel with striking exterior: neat white trim against mustard with hanging flower baskets.

Features two restaurants, a resident's lounge, piano bar, lounge bar, and gardens.

Lochearnhead, *Mansewood Country House.* Telephone: 01567-830213. 6 rooms, all ensuite. Lovely 250-year-old manse surrounded by gardens. Features log fires, charming rooms, and warm atmosphere. Excellent restaurant also on the premises.

Perth, *Achnacarry Guest House,* David and Alison Golder, 3 Pitcullen Crescent. Telephone: 01738-621421. E-mail: info@achnacarry.co.uk. 4 rooms, all ensuite. Although many guesthouses line this street, Achnacarry is one of the nicest and most welcoming ones.

Port of Menteith, *Lake of Menteith Hotel,* Perthshire. Telephone: 01877-385258. Fax: 01877-385671. 16 rooms, all ensuite. Located beside the Lake of Menteith—Scotland's only lake—between the towns of Callander and Aberfoyle off the A81. Family-run. Great opportunities for hill walking, golfing, fishing. The hotel boat is available for fishing. Excellent restaurant too.

Stirling, *Carol Cameron,* 10 Gladstone Place. Telephone: 01786-472681. 3 rooms, all ensuite. Handsome Victorian house, fully modernized, located in quiet residential area of town yet close to the city center and Stirling Castle.

Stirling, *Forth Guest House,* Sheena and Jim Loudon, 23 Forth Place, Riverside. Telephone: 01786-471020. Fax: 01786-447220. 6 rooms, all ensuite. Known for its hanging flower baskets and other delightful touches of color, the Forth boasts a small garden in front and compact but comfortable bedrooms. A short walk from the town center.

Strathyre, *Tony and Christine Ffinch,* Dochfour. Telephone/Fax: 01877-384256. 3 rooms, 2 ensuite. Very charming and cozy Victorian home located in the tiny village of Strathyre. Tony and Christine specialize in home cooking.

ARGYLL & THE ISLANDS

COLL
Arinagour
TIREE
Scarinish

Tobermory
Calgary
Dervaig
TRESHNISH IS.
ULVA
STAFFA
Salen
A849
Fishnish
Craignure
Ben More
▲ 3,169 ft.
A849
Sound of Iona Pennyghael
IONA
Fionnphort
Ross of Mull
Carsaig
MULL

Sound of Mull
A884
A828
LISMORE
Loch Etive
Connel
Ben Cruachan
1,126 ft.
Oban
Taynuilt
A82

Firth of Lorn
SEIL
LUING
KERRERA
Dalmally
A85
A82

ATLANTIC
OCEAN

N

COLONSAY
Scalasaig
JURA
ORONSAY

ISLAY
Port Askaig
A847
Port Charlotte
Bowmore
Portnahaven

SCARBA
Ardfern
Crinan
Sound of Jura
A816
A83
Inveraray
Auchindrain
Arrochar
A83

Kilmartin
A83
Lochgilphead
A886
Garelochhead
A815
A814
A82
OSOK

Loch Awe
Loch Fyne
Helensburgh
Dunoon
A78

PAPS OF JURA
A846
Craighouse
Sound of Islay
A846
A847

Tighnabruaich
Tarbert
BUTE I.
Rothesay
Kennacraig

GREAT
CUMBRAE
LITTLE
CUMBRAE

Firth of Clyde

GIGHA
Ardminish
A83
Claonaig
Catacol
Sound of Bute
Lochranza

Goat Fell
2,866 ft. ▲
Brodick
Machrie
Bay
ARRAN
HOLY ISLAND
Corrie
Brodick Bay
Lamlash

Kintyre
Blackwaterfoot
Machrihanish
Campbeltown
Mull of
Kintyre

Whiting Bay
Kildonan

0   20 miles
0   20 kilometers

ARGYLL
& THE
ISLANDS

Argyll & the Islands

It's often been said that Argyll is where the Highlands meets the Lowlands. For here two distinctive worlds—Lowland bustle and Highland grandeur—come together.

The gateway to the Hebrides is the popular ferry port and resort town of Oban. The town's most famous landmark, which is at its most impressive when viewed from the harbor, is the unfinished McCaig's Tower, or McCaig's Folly, as it is often called. Located on a hill overlooking Oban Bay, it was built by a Mr. McCaig, a local banker with apparently grandiose visions, who seemed determined to bring a piece of the Roman Colosseum to western Scotland. Alas, he died before the ambitious project was completed.

Oban has a festive nightlife in the form of eateries, lively pubs, and Scottish *ceilidhs* (parties), especially at venues such as McTavish's Kitchen, a restaurant by day and club by night. Its Scottish Show continues to pack them in with its combustible combination of daft charm and contagious good spirits. The Gathering Restaurant and Ceilidh Bar on Breadalbane Street is one of the oldest restaurants in Oban. Built in 1882, it specializes in local seafood, Scottish beef, and local game. O'Donnell's Irish Pub, downstairs from the restaurant, features Celtic music and dancing most evenings.

Away from the mainland are several islands that represent the best of Scotland in miniature. The Isle of Arran, one of the Firth of Clyde islands, has been a popular destination for people trying to escape from the daily routine since the nineteenth century. Its sharply defined mountain peaks in the north and rolling hills in the south, combined with charming villages and lovely glens, have helped make Arran a perennial summer favorite for both visitors and natives. The distinctive outline of Goat Fell, at 2,866 feet the highest mountain on the island, may not be tall by world standards, but here it remains the island's best-known natural landmark.

Brodick is the largest settlement on Arran. The Isle of Arran

Heritage Museum, on the outskirts of town, is worth a visit, with its exhibits on island life from the earliest times to the 1920s. Located in Scotland's first and only island country park, the red sandstone Brodick Castle dominates an expansive area that includes a 65-acre woodland garden and eighteenth-century walled garden. Lamlash is a pretty village overlooking Brodick Bay. From the main road extend your gaze to Holy Isle, which houses a community of Tibetan Buddhists who have established a meditation center there.

Two other important Hebridean islands worth closer inspection include Mull and Iona. Tobermory, the biggest town on Mull, is a lovely and peaceful village where small, gaily painted houses hug the harbor. It boasts a fine local history museum, several excellent restaurants, and even its own distillery, and is a good base for exploring the rest of the island.

In the north of the island the pretty little village of Dervaig plays host to reportedly the smallest professional theater in the United Kingdom, the Mull Little Theatre, and it contains 43 seats as proof. While here, take a few minutes to stop by the local museum, the Old Byre Heritage Centre.

Iona has been called the cradle of Scottish Christianity—quite a reputation to maintain for such a tiny island (it's only a mile wide and 3^1/$_2$ miles long, with a permanent population of about 100). And yet Iona looms large in the popular imagination of many a spiritual traveler. For it was here that the Irish scholar-soldier-saint Columba arrived from Ireland in 563 with a dozen disciples to establish a monastery. Fast forward to 1979, when the island was sold to the Fraser Foundation, which then committed a most charitable act—presenting it to the people of Scotland as a gift. Ultimately ownership was transferred to the National Trust for Scotland. Today it remains a popular destination for spiritual and secular travelers alike.

Most visitors stay for only a few hours before catching the ferry back to Mull—a big mistake. To fully capture the flavor, the magic, of the island you should at least stay overnight, and preferably longer. One can spend many pleasant days just wandering around the island, sitting on the white sandy beaches and watching the waves lapping gently against the shoreline, or simply listening to the silence. And if at all possible you should attend an ecumenical service at the Iona Abbey.

Ferry Cottage
Carole and Terry Bennetton
Ardmay
Arrochar
Telephone: 01301-702428
Fax: 01301-702729
E-mail: Ferrycottagebb@aol.com
Web site: www.ferrycottage.com
Bedrooms: 7 rooms, all ensuite.
Rates: £25-35 single. **Credit cards:** VISA, Eurocard, MasterCard, American Express. **Open:** January-November. **Children:** Yes, but none under 2. **Pets:** No. **Smoking:** No. **Provision for handicapped:** No.
Directions: 1 mile south of Arrochar on the A814.

The Ferry Cottage has a nice piece of history attached to it. Originally it was the ferryman's cottage from which the ferry used to run passengers across Loch Long until about 100 years ago. Today the 200-year-old cottage has been completely renovated and is now the Bennetton family home. All rooms have elevated views overlooking the loch. Despite its seemingly remote location—it really isn't that remote—the cottage is a good base for walking and hill climbing the Arrochar Alps. Best of all, it's only a five-minute drive from the legendary braes of Loch Lomond. And after a long day's journey trudging the hills and dales, it's reassuring to know that a hearty dinner awaits you. Top off the evening with a restful sleep. Ferry Cottage is situated in Scotland's first national park, Loch Lomond National Park.

Iona Cottage
Carol Kirkpatrick
Isle of Iona
Telephone/Fax: 01681-700358
Bedrooms: 4 rooms, all with shared bath.
Rates: £25-27.50 pp. **Credit cards:** None. **Open:** Mid-March to September-October. **Children:** Yes. **Pets:** No. **Smoking:** No. **Provision for handicapped:** No. **Directions:** The ferry from Oban to the Isle of Mull takes about 40 minutes. It takes about one hour to drive through Mull (there is also regular bus service available), and then a 10-minute ferry ride to Iona (no cars are allowed on the island). The cottage is about 100 yards from the ferry terminal.

This family-run B&B is housed in a charming 200-year-old cottage, just steps away from the lovely beach. The cottage is only a 10-minute walk from the Iona Abbey, the spiritual center of the island. What's more, it's also very convenient to the ferry terminal, standing as it does on a shallow rise facing the jetty. In the 1840s the cottage functioned as the island's original pub (a photograph of it in its earlier incarnation is on display in the local history museum). Its three rooms face the sea, and an open fire warms visitors in the cozy sitting room. Relax and unwind amid its beautifully restored interior. Dinners typically consist of three courses followed by tea or coffee. During mealtimes guests share their meals in the sun lounge, which overlooks the Sound of Iona. All in all, it's a charming and peaceful kind of place—the kind of place you would expect to find on this most sacred of isles. Bicycle rentals can be arranged. For those on a healthy diet, please note that the staff specializes in vegetarian cooking.

Balmoral Inn
Constantine Pilavachi
4 Craigard Road
Oban
Telephone: 01631-562731
Fax: 01631-566810
E-mail: enquiries@balmoraloban.co.uk
Web site: www.balmoraloban.co.uk
Bedrooms: 9 rooms, 9 ensuite.
Rates: From £25-30 pp. **Credit cards:** VISA, MasterCard, Delta, Solo.
Open: Except Christmas. **Children:** Yes. **Pets:** Yes. **Smoking:** In rooms
only. **Provision for handicapped:** No. **Directions:** Located near Oban's
pier, just off the town's main thoroughfare, George Street.

The Balmoral is efficiently run by the new owner, Constantine
Pilavachi. In addition, Constantine carries a very nice selection of fine
wines and single malt whiskies. The ambiance throughout is informal
and casual, the staff friendly and helpful. Balmoral is located near the
pier and Oban's major attractions, yet is discreetly tucked away on a
quiet side street far enough away from the noise—and being a port
town, make no mistake about it, Oban can get quite rowdy at times—
that it's safe to say that it offers the best of both worlds. Balmoral is a
popular place in season—make sure you book in advance.

Glenbervie Guest House
Iain and Joan Auld
Dalriach Road
Oban
Telephone: 01631-564770
Fax: 01631-566723
E-mail: glenbervie@lineone.com
Bedrooms: 8 rooms, all ensuite or with private facilities.
Rate: £18-25 double. **Credit cards:** No. **Open:** All year. **Children:** Yes.
Pets: No. **Smoking:** No. **Provision for handicapped:** No. **Directions:**
From George Street take Dunollie Road to Dalriach Road.

Glenbervie boasts a great location. Perched high above Oban, it offers outstanding views of the surrounding landscape, a marvelous vista of mountains, sea, and open sky. It also happens to be one of the cleanest and most comfortable B&Bs I've had the pleasure of visiting in recent years. The décor is bright and cheery throughout, and your hosts, Iain and Joan, quietly do their best to be more than accommodating, even when this means doing something beyond the call of duty. During a visit, I was bogged down by one too many bags and wished to make a two-day trip to Mull and Iona; the Aulds were kind enough to safeguard my luggage. Such nice touches add immeasurably to the B&B experience. Glenbervie is also convenient to the town center. A word of warning though: Dalriach Road is winding and steep. If you have heavy luggage or luggage without wheels, it is best to take a taxi from the rail station—it will cost you a few pounds, but it's worth it in the long run.

Failte Guest House
Mairi Barlow
Main Street
Tobermory
Isle of Mull
Telephone/Fax: 01688-302495
E-mail: barlow@tob302495.freeserve.co.uk
Bedrooms: 7 rooms, all ensuite.
Rates: £22 double. **Credit cards:** VISA, MasterCard. **Open:** March to
October. **Children:** Yes. **Pets:** No. **Smoking:** No. **Provision for handicapped:** No. **Directions:** On the main road of the town.

Failte is one of the most attractive B&Bs in town. It boasts a great
location on the main road looking across Tobermory Bay. Moreover, it
presents a warm beige exterior to the world that, on a bright day,
almost basks in the warmth of the sun. Inside, the interior is cozy and
spotlessly clean. Tobermory itself is a handsome town, with several
noteworthy attractions of its own. A short walk along the main street at
the southern end of the harbor will bring you to the Tobermory
Distillery (there's a visitor's center and shop), while in the opposite
direction lies a small but fascinating local history museum. I find that
knowing something about the history of the place where I'm staying
adds considerably to my visit, and since Mull has such a long and complex past, it comes highly recommended. If history is not your cup of
tea, not to worry. There are two nine-hole golf courses on the island,
one at Craignure and the other in Tobermory itself.

Highland Cottage
Dave and Jo Currie
Breadalbane Street
Tobermory
Isle of Mull
Telephone: 01688-302030
Fax: 01688-302727
E-mail: davidandjo@highlandcottage.co.uk
Bedrooms: 6 rooms, all ensuite, including 2 with fourposter beds.
Rates: £29.50-45 double. **Credit cards:** VISA, MasterCard. **Open:** Year-round. **Children:** Yes. **Pets:** Well-behaved pets only. **Smoking:** Sun lounge and sitting room only. **Provision for handicapped:** Yes.
Directions: When you reach Tobermory from the Craignure or Fishnish ferries at the roundabout, take the road straight ahead, crossing the narrow stone bridge. Take the first turn right and follow the road round until it opens out. Highland Cottage is the building on the right, opposite the fire station.

Dave Currie, a former training director with Sheraton Hotels in Europe, and his wife, Josephine, ran a successful hotel near Windsor Castle for 16 years. But they wanted something more, and their eyes looked northward, across the border. So together they conceived and built Highland Cottage—a spanking-new building set to traditional cottage design. It opened in April 1998 in a quiet area of Upper Tobermory's historic district. This is a first-rate place from top to bottom—your own home away from home. Beautifully and tastefully decorated, each room is named and given a theme after a different Scottish island. Most bedrooms come furnished with antique or fourposter beds.

The fresh local ingredients are imaginatively cooked and presented. Dinner consists of four courses with coffee for £21.50. A typical meal begins with a melon accompanied by homemade pear sorbet or venison followed by Tobermory smoked salmon and trout roulade. Then take your pick of cream of carrot, tomato, or coriander soup. The main entrée is a delightful feast: roast stuffed breast of chicken or perhaps local scallops with ginger cream. To conclude, try the poached pear with homemade cinnamon ice cream. There's also an extensive collection of books available for browsing on those rainy nights when nursing a Tobermory single malt seems like the right thing to do. All in all, this is a wonderful place to recharge your batteries.

Clachaig Inn
Guy and Edward Daynes
Glencoe
Argyll
Telephone: 01855-811252
Fax: 01855-812030
E-mail: inn@clachaig.com
Web site: www.clachaig.com
Bedrooms: 23, all ensuite.
Rates: £32-42 per person. **Credit cards:** MasterCard and VISA. **Open:** All year except Christmas. **Children:** Yes. Welcome in the Lounge Bar but not in the Public Bar. **Pets:** Yes (£2.50 per night additional surcharge). **Smoking:** Yes. **Provision for handicapped:** Some rooms are on the ground floor although none are suitable for wheelchair use. **Directions:** Situated half a mile off the main A82 road that passes through the glen. The inn is clearly signposted.

An old drover's inn in the historic Glencoe area, Clachaig Inn has an informal and rustic atmosphere. It houses two large bars, the public bar to the rear and the lounge bar in the front, which offers spectacular views of Aonach Dubh, Glencoe's most foreboding peak. The Clachaig Inn is probably best known for its traditional "real" ales, with up to nine (and occasionally more) on handpull at any one time. Most are from small independent Scottish breweries, such as Atlas, Cairngorm, Skye, Orkney, Hebridean, and Williams Brothers. *Les Routiers* named the Clachaig Inn their Real Ale Pub of the Year 2004. Over 100 single malt whiskies are on tap. Self-catering chalets are also available.

ALSO RECOMMENDED

Arden, *Auchenheglish Lodge,* Mr. G. Wylie, Lomond Castle. Telephone/Fax: 01389-850688. 3 rooms, 2 ensuite. Includes a private beach and slipway on Loch Lomond. Boat rental available.

Balloch, *Station Cottages,* Marie and Eamonn McAteer, Balloch Road. Telephone: 01389-750759. Fax: 01389-710501. 2 rooms, both ensuite. Former Victorian station cottages minutes away from Loch Lomond, hotels, and restaurants.

Ballygrant, *Kilmeny Farmhouse,* Margaret Rozga, Isle of Islay. Telephone/Fax: 01496-840668. Web site: www.isleofslay.com/group/guest/kilmeny. 3 rooms, all ensuite. Attractive whitewashed farmhouse with a fine reputation for excellent food and service.

Brodick, *Dunvegan House,* Isle of Arran, David and Naomi Spencer, Shore Road. Telephone: 01770-302811. Ideally located on Brodick's seafront. David and Naomi take a personal interest in ensuring their guests are made comfortable. An excellent dinner is offered in the evenings.

Dervaig, *Cuin Lodge,* David and Dorothy Aitken. Telephone: 01688-400346. 4 rooms, 2 ensuite. Traditional nineteenth-century shooting lodge located one mile from the village of Dervaig.

Isle of Iona, *Argyll Hotel,* Daniel Morgan and Claire Bachellerie, Isle of Iona. Telephone: 01681-700334. Fax: 01681-700510. E-mail: reception@argyllhoteliona.co.uk. 17 rooms; 15 ensuite and 2 singles with shared bath. Comfortable and simple converted croft house located near Iona Abbey. Savor the cozy lounges with open fires, elegant dining room, and greenhouse. Good reputation for using fresh local ingredients. Vegetarian and wholefood dishes are served.

Lamlash, *Glenisle Hotel,* Fred and Liz, Isle of Arran. Telephone: 01770-600559. All 13 rooms ensuite. Small and cheery country B&B. Tastefully decorated. The large garden and many of the rooms have sea views across Lamlash Bay toward Holy Isle. Excellent restaurant on the premises, too.

Oban, *Hawthornbank Guest House,* Colin and Isobel McLachlan, Dalriach Road. Telephone: 01631-562041. 8 rooms, 7 ensuite. Victorian villa overlooking Oban Bay. Features fourposter and brass beds.

THE HIGHLANDS

HIGHLAND

0   5 miles

0   5 kilometers

N

Pentland Firth

STROMA ISLAND

John o'Groa

Dunnet Head

Dunnet

Mey

Canisbe

Scrabster

Auckengill

Keiss

Sinclair Bay

Thurso

Reay

Melvich

Halkirk

Wick

Cape Wrath

Balnakeil

Strathy Point

Strathy

Bettyhill

Dunnet

CAITHNES

Ulbster

Whaligoe

Durness

Kyle of Tongue

Tongue

Loch Loyal

Dunbeath

Latheron

Badbea

Kinlochbervie

Loch Hope

Syre

Rosal

Flow Country

Forsinard

Berriedale

HANDA ISLAND

Laxford Bridge

Loch Naver

Kinbrace

Kildonan

Helmsdale

Scourie

Altnaharra

Strath of Kildonan

Drumbeg

Kylesku

SUTHERLAND

Stoer

Loch Assynt

Inchnadamph

Loch Shin

Lairg

Rogart

Brora

Lochinver

Inverkirkaig

Elphin

Glen Oykel

Oykel Bridge

Bonar Bridge

Spinningdale

Golspie

Achiltibuie

Loch Broom

Dornoch

SUMMER ISLES

Little Loch Broom

Ullapool

Inveran

Croick

Ardgay

Dornoch Firth

Portmahomack

Poolewe

Dundonnell

Glencalvie Forest

Tain

Moray Firth

Gairloch

Loch Maree

Invergordon

Alness

Nigg

Cromarty

ROSS AND CROMARTY

Evanton

Dingwall

Fortrose

Nairn

Kinlochewe

Achnasheen

Torridon

Strath Conon

Strathpeffer

Cawdor

Shieldaig

Applecross

Muir of Ord

Beauly

Inverness

Lochcarron

Strathcarron

Abriachan

Plockton

Stromeferry

Cannich

Glen Urquhart

Drumnadrochit

Grantown on Spey

Kyle of Lochalsh

Dornie

Carrbridge

ISLE OF SKYE

Glenelg

Shiel Bridge

INVERNESS

Boat of Garten

Glen Shiel

Invermoriston

Aviemore

KNOYDART

Inverie

Glen Moriston

Fort Augustus

Kingussie

Loch Quoich

Loch Arisaig

Invergarry

Newtonmore

STRATHSPEY

Mallaig

Morar

Loch Morar

Gairlochy

Roy Bridge

Dalwhinnie

Arisaig

LOCHABER

Spean Bridge

EIGG

Lochailort

Ben Nevis 4,406 ft.

Acharacle

MOIDART

Fort William

Sanna

ARDNAMURCHAN

Onich

Kinlochleven

Salen

Strontian

Glencoe

Blackwater res.

Ballachulish

Glen Coe

Kingshouse

INVERNESS AREA

Evanton

Cromarty

Dingwall

Fortrose

Rosemarkie

Strathpeffer

Avoch

North Kessock

Muir of Ord

Cawdor

Beauly

Beauly Firth

Inverness Firth

Inverness

The Highlands

The Scotland that people imagine is the Scotland of the Highlands. The Scotland of ominous mountains breaking through a blanket of clouds; the Scotland of shimmering loch after shimmering loch; the Scotland of the world's romantic literature. The Scotland of the mind.

But there is quite a lot of truth to be discovered in this Scotland of the mind. The sights that you have seen in postcards, coffee table books, and Hollywood movies really do exist. And yet the Highlands is an exceedingly vast and complex land. To reduce it to a few stock shots culled from the Hollywood image factory is to do it a tremendous disservice. There are in fact many Highlands. Let's look at a few of them.

Caithness is the most northerly county in Britain. Much of the interior is decidedly flat. The biggest towns in this northern land are Wick and Thurso, whose names reflect their Scandinavian origins.

Ben Nevis, Britain's tallest mountain, is located in wild Lochaber, as is gorgeous Glen Nevis, considered by some to be the most beautiful glen in Scotland. It certainly appealed to the Hollywood set, since both *Braveheart* and *Rob Roy* were partially shot here.

Inverness is the largest city in the Highlands—actually the *only* city in the Highlands. With a population of approximately 60,000 for the greater metropolitan area, Inverness earns its accolade as the capital of the Highlands by dint of population alone. And as expected in a capital city, it boasts a thriving cultural scene, including the Eden Court Theatre.

Further north, beyond Inverness, lies Sutherland, the least densely populated area in Europe, which stretches across much of the broad expanse of northern Scotland. Here you will find, especially in the remote northwest, the Highlands of legend. It is a brooding landscape, empty, forlorn in parts, so bleakly beautiful that it leaves you wide-eyed and speechless. It is a swirling combination of foreboding mountains, lochs, and low-lying clouds.

Old Library Lodge & Restaurant
Mike and Jilly Jones
Main Road
Arisaig
Telephone: 01687-450651
Fax: 01687-450219
Bedrooms: 6 rooms, all ensuite.
Rates: £35-45 pp. **Credit cards:** VISA, Delta, MasterCard, JCB,
Eurocard, Switch. **Open:** Easter to late October. **Children:** Yes. **Pets:**
No. **Smoking:** No. **Provision for handicapped:** No. **Directions:** Located
along the main road of the village of Arisaig.

Arisaig offers one of the finest meals and accommodations in this
part of the Highlands—hands-down. Located in the center of the tiny
village of Arisaig, smack on the waterfront, it is run with great aplomb
by Mike and Jilly Jones. Their small traditional-style restaurant offers
good food with spectacular views. From its windows you can enjoy, in
good weather, excellent views over to the Small Isles, especially the
unusual rock formation known as An Sgurr on the Isle of Eigg (there
is a private ferry service to Eigg and the other Small Isles from Arisaig
during the season).

The building itself is over 200 years old, a stone-built stable converted to a restaurant. The accommodation is equally impressive, especially the modern addition that consists of a wing of terraced rooms
with balconies overlooking a lovely garden. The bright and vibrant colors recall more of a Mediterranean seafront resort than the western
Highlands of Scotland. For those interested in a bit of Highland literary history, the great Gaelic poet Alexander MacDonald was born near

here in 1698. He is buried in an Arisaig graveyard in an unknown plot. A plaque sponsored by Highland Regional Council and Scottish Natural Heritage provides biographical information. The Land, Sea, and Islands Centre, located along Arisaig's main road, celebrates the social and natural history of the area.

Craigellachie House
Terry and Shan Dudleston
Main Street
Carrbridge
Telephone: 01479-841641
Fax: 0149-841415
E-mail: craigellachiehouse@fsmail.net
Web site: www.carrbridge.com
Bedrooms: 5 rooms, 3 ensuite, 2 with private shower rooms.
Rates: £21-23 pp. **Credit cards:** VISA, MasterCard, Delta, Switch, Solo.
Open: All year. **Children:** Yes. **Pets:** No. **Smoking:** No. **Provision for handicapped:** No. **Directions:** Carrbridge is 2 miles off the main A9 road. The guesthouse is situated on the main street through the village.

A warm and friendly Victorian house set in the center of the village, Craigellachie is individually decorated. Some rooms have ensuite facilities, but all come with wash/hand basin, tea- and coffee-making facilities, and central heating. Relax in the informal and comfortable resident's lounge and dining room—the owners stock local and Speyside malts—complete with log fires. The varied menu makes the best of local Scottish produce as well as herbs taken from their own garden. Attractions in the area are varied: golfing and fishing on the River Spey are two activities, as well as birdwatching and pony-trekking. There are also many distilleries in the area. Since Craigellachie is located in the heart of the Cairngorms, skiing is a popular pastime in the winter. Walkers and cyclists are warmly welcomed too.

2 Quail Restaurant and Rooms
Michael and Kerensa Carr
Castle Street
Dornoch
Sutherland
Telephone: 01862-811263
Bedrooms: 2 rooms; 1 ensuite, 1 with private facilities.
Rates: £80-100 double/twin. **Credit cards:** Yes. **Open:** All year.
Children: No children under 10. **Pets:** No. **Smoking:** In lounge only.
Provision for handicapped: No. **Directions:** Just off the A9 north of
Inverness, along Dornoch's main street.

This B&B is a real find. Who would have thought that such a sophisticated restaurant and lovely accommodations could be found on the main road in this quiet northern Highland village? Yet here it is, a traditional Highland townhouse with a cozy lounge, where you can either listen to music or read books. Many people stumble across it—and what a pleasant surprise they have in store for them. Just glancing at the three-course dinner menu of the 2 Quail Restaurant (07000-2QUAIL or 01862-811811) is enough to make your mouth water: scallop risotto with beans and crispy bacon, roast loin of venison with brandied cherries and thyme sauce, or supreme of turbot with an orange crust and a fricassé of cherry tomatoes and basil. And for dessert, dark and white chocolate pavé with mint sauce. The menu changes weekly, so you'll never be sure exactly what you're going to get. Be assured that whatever is offered it will be memorable.

The tasteful décor adds to the soothing and civilized atmosphere. Tables are spread out among two tartan-clad dining rooms surrounded by book-lined shelves and warm, yellowish wallpaper. (The restaurant is open from Tuesday to Saturday for dinner, from 7:30-9:30 P.M.) Upstairs are several comfortable bedrooms, tastefully decorated, and surrounded by natural-grain wood. The Carrs, newcomers to the area from the north of England, opened 2 Quail in 1998 (it was originally called Inistore Guest House). Michael is the chef; Kerensa personally reviews and updates the wine list (about 70 offerings at last count). This B&B is a real winner over all.

Trevose Guest House
Jean Mackenzie
The Square
Dornoch
Sutherland
Telephone: 01862-810269
E-mail: trevose@amserve.net
Bedrooms: 4 rooms, 2 ensuite.
Rates: £45. **Credit cards:** No. **Open:** March to mid-October. **Children:** Yes. **Pets:** Dogs welcome. **Smoking:** No. **Provision for handicapped:** No. **Directions:** Trevose is located directly across the street from Dornoch Cathedral, in the center of town.

Trevose is a perfectly pleasant B&B, ideally located in the center of town. Indeed, you really couldn't ask for a more ideal setting. It overlooks the village green and is across the street from lovely Dornoch Cathedral. Do have a peek inside. It's small but impressive. One particular stained-glass window has special appeal in this part of Scotland, dedicated as it is in "loving memory of A. Carnegie of Skibo 1835-1919." The wealthy Scottish American Andrew Carnegie lived in nearby Skibo Castle for many years. (Nowadays the castle houses the Carnegie Club, a private residential golf and sporting club with an international membership limited by invitation.) Trevose itself is an attractive sandstone building, dating back to 1830.

When you first arrive, and if it is a nice day, you will probably see Jean Mackenzie puttering around in the garden. The garden is a lovely one too, full of wonderful splashes of color. Jean herself is a handsome and reserved woman but very kindhearted. Dornoch has a number of nearby attractions. The famous Royal Dornoch golf course is just a five minute walk away. Also within the vicinity are salmon and trout fishing, as well as game shooting and pony-trekking. There are many opportunities to enjoy invigorating coastal walks and fine sandy beaches. Indeed, Dornoch boasts some of the finest beaches in Scotland. Because of its northern latitude though, you won't find too many people dipping into the water.

The Lodge at Daviot Mains
Margaret and Alex Hutcheson
Daviot Mains Farm
Near Inverness
Telephone: 01463-772215
Fax: 01463-772099
E-mail: info@thelodge-daviotmains.co.uk
Web site: www.thelodgeatdaviotmains.co.uk
Bedrooms: 7 rooms, all ensuite.
Rates: £35-37 single, £30-35 double/twin. **Credit cards:** MasterCard,
VISA. **Open:** Year-round except Christmas Eve and Christmas Day.
Children: Yes; discounts for children under 12 sharing room with two
adults. **Pets:** Dogs by arrangement. **Smoking:** No. **Provision for hand-
icapped:** Yes. **Directions:** Located on the B851 road just off the main
A9, about 6 miles south of Inverness. Take the B851 to Croy. The farm
is .75 mile further along.

Daviot is an early-nineteenth-century farmhouse located in a quiet
area near Inverness. It offers an unusual design: four wings enclose a
central courtyard. The immaculately clean bedrooms are all named
after nearby rivers. The Hutchesons have been entertaining guests for
more than 20 years now, and their enthusiasm shows no signs of abat-
ing. Indeed, they have made many lasting friendships over the years,
especially among Americans, "and now," says Margaret, "have a lengthy
Christmas card list over the water." Homemade goodies—scones and
shortbread—are offered as a "nightcap." Dinner is also quite special
here (£19-21.50 pp.). Traditional Scottish dishes that may appear on
your plate include fresh, locally caught salmon and trout, Scottish lamb
and Aberdeen Angus beef, vegetables, cheeses, and seasonal fruits.
Enjoy the comfy sitting room in front of the log fire. The Lodge also
features direct-dial phone and Internet access in all rooms.

The Osprey Hotel
Robert and Aileen Burrow
Ruthven Road
Kingussie
Telephone/Fax: 01540-661510
E-mail: aileen@ospreyhotel.freeserve.co.uk
Web site: www.ospreyhotel.co.uk
Bedrooms: 8 rooms; all ensuite.
Rates: £29-36 single/double; £49-56 with dinner. **Credit cards:**
MasterCard, VISA. **Open:** All year. **Children:** Yes. **Pets:** Well-behaved
dogs. **Smoking:** No. **Provision for handicapped:** No, but 2 bedrooms
are on the ground floor. **Directions:** Located on the southern por-
tion of Kingussie, just off the main A9 trunk road; about 300 meters
from the main Inverness to London main station.

The Osprey is a small hotel overlooking the Memorial Gardens in
the center of the Highland village of Kingussie. Informal yet elegant,
the personal touch of owners Robert and Aileen is evident everywhere, from the tasteful décor to the elegant meals. Red-carpeted hallways make for a truly warm welcome. The eight pretty rooms are quiet
and cozy and come with private facilities, color television, clock
radio/alarm, refreshment tray, electric blanket, and hair dryer. After
dinner, relax in one of their two lounges and choose from a nicely
chosen selection of malt whisky, port, brandy, or liqueur.
Evening meals are among the best in town. Specialties include
prime beef, venison, game, salmon, and trout. All are imaginatively
presented with a certain flair: pecan and apple soup with a hint of
curry for starters, salmon with leek and tarragon as the entrée, and for

dessert chocolate and orange roulade, followed by coffee and mints. The Burrows also offer an excellent selection of European country wines as well as wines from Australia, New Zealand, North and South America, and South Africa. The breakfast menu typically consists of porridge, oak-smoked haddock and kippers, local heather honey, and freshly ground coffee. The breads and rolls are baked daily in their own kitchen.

Sonnhalde
Janis and Bernie Jones
East Terrace
Kingussie
Telephone: 01540-661266
E-mail: sonn.gh@btopenworld.com
Bedrooms: 7 rooms, 3 ensuite.
Rates: From £18 pp., dinner and B&B from £27. **Credit cards:** No.
Open: Year-round. **Children:** Yes. **Pets:** No. **Smoking:** In lounge only.
Provision for handicapped: Yes. **Directions:** Approaching the village
traffic lights from the south, turn left. Then make a right turn into
East Terrace. Sonnhalde is the third house on the left.

Bernie Jones is full of rambunctious energy and he's a keen pho-
tographer to boot (he also runs a photo studio called B+J
Photography). Bernie and his wife Janis run this spic-and-span B&B,
which is located up a steep incline, with wonderful views across the
Spey Valley to the Ruthven Barracks ruins and the Cairngorm mountains beyond. The name means "Sunnybank"—it's located on a bank,
sometimes sunny, sometimes not, just above High Street beside the
town clock.
The rooms in this 100-year-old building are spacious and comfortable, the décor warm. The hanging plants reflect Bernie's love of
nature. He is also an avid birdwatcher, and this energetic
Yorkshireman is glad to offer nature and photographic tours (including field trips and darkroom and studio use) to the area's glens and
surrounding countryside. While in town you must stop by the excellent Highland Folk Museum on Duke Street. The highlight of the
museum's collections is most certainly the Isle of Lewis Blackhouse, a

replica of a traditional thatched Highland dwelling.

For a relaxing bite to eat, check out Gilly's Kitchen along High Street, which offers a surprisingly sophisticated menu for a small café: Rannoch smoked venison paté with toast, couscous potato salad, or baguettes and croissants with roasted vegetables in olive oil.

Culduthel Lodge
David and Marion Bonsor
14 Culduthel Road
Inverness
Telephone/Fax: 01463-240089
E-mail: enquiry@culduthel.com
Bedrooms: 12 rooms, all ensuite.
Rates: From £45 single, from £42.50 double. **Credit cards:** VISA,
MasterCard. **Open:** Year-round. **Children:** 10 and older **Pets:** By
arrangement. **Smoking:** Most rooms are non-smoking. **Provision for
handicapped:** No. **Directions:** Located along Culduthel Road, a short
drive off Inverness's High Street.

My vote for the best accommodations in Inverness goes to the
Culduthel. David and Marion Bonsor offer the best in Highland hospitality and graciousness. This Georgian beauty is located in an attrac-
tively upscale section of Inverness, a short walk away from the River
Ness, and set on its own grounds. The traditional drawing room has
large windows that look out over Inverness and the surrounding hills.
On arrival, guests will appreciate several small and thoughtful touches:
fresh fruit, a small decanter of sherry, and a CD/cassette/radio player.
Among the other services are 24-hour laundry service and a complimentary daily newspaper of your choice. In pleasant weather, enjoy a
glass of wine or a cup of tea on the outdoor terrace. David, your tall
and handsome host, will likely be the one serving your morning coffee
or full Scottish breakfast. Drinks and light snacks are available until
midnight in the drawing room, your bedroom, or on the terrace. A
homey fixture of Culduthel Lodge is the sight of Shelly, the family
dog, reclining lazily in all her glory in the hallway or by the door.
Culduthel may be a first-class lodge, but it still offers its down-home
touches—thank goodness.

East Dene Guest House
Phyllis and Don Greig
6 Ballifeary Road
Inverness
Telephone/Fax: 01463-232976
E-mail: dgreig@nildram.co.uk
Web site: www.SmoothHound.co.uk/hotels/eastd.html
Bedrooms: 4 rooms; 3 ensuite, 1 room with private bathroom.
Rates: £24-28. **Credit cards:** VISA and MasterCard. **Open:** Year-round.
Children: 12 and up. **Pets:** No. **Smoking:** Restricted. **Provision for handicapped:** No. **Directions:** Situated on the north side of the River Ness, close to Eden Court Theatre, between Glenurquhart Road (A82) and the Ness Walk.

The Greig's children were brought up in this traditional stone-built Victorian house. Their departure made the place feel cold and empty, so Don and Phyllis, given their gregarious nature, did the most logical thing they could think of—they invited the world to stay with them. The rooms are tastefully decorated, the lounge comfortable. East Dene is conveniently located less than 10 minutes from the town center. Also nearby are numerous golf courses, bowling greens, tennis and squash courts, fishing, and other leisure and recreational facilities. St. Andrews Cathedral is also within walking distance.

Ivy Bank Guest House
Catherine Cameron
28 Old Edinburgh Road
Inverness
Telephone/Fax: 01463-232796
E-mail: invybankiv@talk21.com
Web site: www.ivybankguesthouse.com
Bedrooms: 6 rooms, 3 ensuite, 1 with private facilities.
Rates: From £25. **Credit cards:** MasterCard, VISA. **Open:** Year-round.
Children: Yes. **Pets:** Yes. **Smoking:** No. **Provision for handicapped:** No.
Directions: From the A82, continue across the bridge, up Castle
Street. The guesthouse is at the top of the hill.

Built in 1836, this historic Georgian building is full of great character and charm. The interior design reeks of the warmth of another
era: oak paneling, mahogany staircase, open fires, and original fireplaces. Ivy Bank is located within a five minute walk to the town center.
The tastefully decorated lounge is a wonderful place to relax, watch
television, or, should the mood possess you, even play a few chords
on the baby grand piano. The ensuite bedrooms have bath and
shower facilities, and one ensuite room has a fourposter bed. Adding
to the charm is a walled and landscaped garden and pond. Overall, Ivy
Bank is an enjoyable place to unwind and savor life's little pleasures.

Trafford Bank
Lorraine Freel and Koshal Pun
96 Fairfield Road
Inverness
Telephone: 01463-241414
E-mail: info@traffordbankhotel.co.uk
Web site: www.traffordbankhotel.co.uk
Bedrooms: 5, all ensuite.
Rates: £45-55 single pp., £35-44 double pp. **Credit cards:** American
Express, MasterCard, VISA. **Open:** All year. **Children:** Yes. **Pets:** Only
guide dogs all year and small dogs off peak (from November-
February). **Smoking:** No. **Provision for handicapped:** Disabled ramp
into house but no ground floor bedrooms. **Directions:** From the A9
driving north, turn left at the Longman Roundabout. Follow the A82
Tourist Route signs to Fort William.

Trafford Bank recently was awarded five red diamonds by the BAA.
This former bishop's house has been completely renovated by new
owners Lorraine Freel and Koshal Pun. Lorraine, an interior designer,
mixes antique and contemporary furniture. The house itself is surrounded by gardens, which gives the place a serene feel. All rooms
come with flat- screen TV and DVD player, CD player, hospitality tray,
sherry decanter, and hair dryer. The Tartan Room features a large
Victorian-style rolled bathtub. Since Trafford Bank is located in a residential area that can be tricky to navigate, especially for first timers
to Inverness, it probably is best to get specific directions from Lorraine
and Koshal themselves, or check their web site.

Roadstead Bed & Breakfast
Jean Crocket
1 Loch Nevis Crescent
Mallaig
Telephone: 01687-462171
Bedrooms: 2 rooms with private facilities.
Rates: £16 pp. **Credit cards:** No. **Open:** April-October. **Children:** Yes.
Pets: No. **Smoking:** No. **Provision for handicapped:** No. **Directions:**
Proceed through Mallaig until you reach the fire station. Roadstead
is opposite the station.

Jean Crocket is a tiny wisp of a woman, and the perfect Highland
host. Not only does she make you feel an instant member of the
household, she makes sure everyone else is happy and content too.
As soon as you arrive, your quick-footed and diminutive host wastes no
time in offering you a cup of tea and biscuits in the wood-paneled
lounge. And if you happen to be traveling alone and other guests are
staying as well, she takes great pleasure in turning strangers into
acquaintances. No eating in silence while at the Crocket residence.
She and her husband, Andrew, both of whom are retired, take great
pleasure in sharing their home with the rest of the world. The utterly
charming white stucco house is hard to miss: it's the one with the garden out front decorated with miniature windmills, trolls, sea otters,
and other delightful knickknacks. The rooms are exceedingly lovely
and cozy; the views across Mallaig Harbor are splendid. But most of all
it is Jean's warmth that you will most likely take away with you.

Tigh-na-Clash Guest House
Joan and Ian Ritchie
81 Melvich
By Thurso
Sutherland
Telephone/Fax: 01641-531262
E-mail: info@tighnaclash@co.uk
Web site: www.mywebpage.net/tighnaclash
Bedrooms: 7 rooms, all ensuite.
Rates: £24 pp. **Credit cards:** No. **Open:** April-October. **Children:** Yes.
Pets: No. **Smoking:** No smoking in bedrooms or dining room.
Provision for handicapped: No. **Directions:** Tigh-na-Clash is the first
B&B on the left heading north from Helmsdale, opposite the
Halladale Inn.

Located in the small coastal Sutherland village of Melvich in
Scotland's remote north, Tigh-na-Clash offers modern lodging at its
finest. All rooms come with television, tea-making facilities, and the like.
What sets it apart from other accommodations is the personal touch of
the Ritchies. They do their best to make their guests feel comfortable, as
if they had just arrived home from a long journey. It doesn't hurt either
that wonderful views can be observed from the resident's lounge.
The Ritchies offer an immaculate house as well as an attractive garden. Breakfast is a bit on the unusual side too. In addition to the
standard items, they have also added smoked haddock and kippers
to the selections.
    The nearest towns are Thurso and Scrabster, where you can catch
the ferry to Orkney. Also in the vicinity is John O'Groats. Although

little more than a tourist trap, many people who make the effort to venture this far north can't resist coming here, the northernmost settlement on the Scottish mainland. Much wilder is Cape Wrath. Ask the Ritchies for the best way to get there. Alternatively, Sutherland is a nature lover's paradise. Here you are in the heart of Flow Country, a watery wilderness of peatlands, and the RSPB Reserve at Forsinard. Birdwatching and hill walking are just some of the more popular activities up here. But, in good weather, there are also plenty of beaches to enjoy (given the temperature of the water, bathing is not recommended, though), fishing, surfing, and even diving (not for the timid).

Nearby museums include the Timespan Museum in Helmsdale and the Strathnaver Museum at Bettyhill. Both have significant displays on the Highland Clearances. Again, ask the Ritchies for their seasoned advice.

The Sheiling Guest House
Joan and Hugh Campbell
Melvich
North Sutherland
By Thurso
Telephone/Fax: 01641-531256
E-mail: thesheiling@btinternet.com
Web site: www.host.co.uk
Bedrooms: 3 rooms, all ensuite.
Rates: £22-24. **Credit cards:** None. **Open:** March-November. **Children:** Yes. **Pets:** By arrangement only. **Smoking:** No. **Provision for handicapped:** No. **Directions:** Drive north on the A9. Catch the A897 at Helmsdale for 40 miles. Turn left onto the A836 coastal junction. The Sheiling is 2 miles further along.

The Sheiling serves as an excellent base to tour Caithness and Sutherland and to make that day trip across the Pentland Firth to Orkney. Your Sutherland-born hosts bring with them some 30 years of experience in the tourist industry. Their home is situated on 15 acres of hill-crofting ground. Besides the gorgeous views up this way, the real reason to stay at the Sheiling is to savor the terrific breakfasts.

A buffet table includes orange and grapefruit juice, a variety of cold cereals, unusual fruit compotes (rhubarb and melon, banana and orange, fresh raspberries and strawberries), porridge, and homemade yogurt with fruit preserves. Grilled items could include wild brown trout or fresh herring dipped in oatmeal, natural oak-smoked haddock with poached egg, smoked salmon, Aberdeen kippers, or French toast with peppered tomatoes. Also on hand for this bountiful feast are various breads and Scottish oatcakes with homemade jams (rhubarb, lemon curd, plum, gooseberry, black currant, strawberry, and raspberry).

The Campbells have two comfy lounges: the television lounge overlooks Melvich Bay; the sitting room, which faces west and overlooks the garden, is the place to read or play board games. The Campells' motto is simple: "We are here for your pleasure . . . our home is your home."

Sunny Brae Hotel
Sylvia and Ian Bochel
Marine Road
Nairn
Telephone: 01667-452309
Fax: 01667-454860
E-mail: enquiries@runnybraehotel.com
Web site: www.sunnybraehotel.co.uk
Bedrooms: 9 rooms, all ensuite.
Rates: £79-99 single, £47-57 double. **Credit cards:** VISA and MasterCard. **Open:** March-November. **Children:** Well-behaved children only. **Pets:** By arrangement only. **Smoking:** No. **Provision for handicapped:** No, but they have five ground-floor rooms. **Directions:** From Inverness take the roundabout on the A96. Go to the first exit, and then proceed straight ahead for another 350 yards.

Nairn has been a resort town for decades, and Sylvia, who is German, and Ian do their best to encourage visitors to take full advantage of the many attractions in the vicinity. From the lounge, dining room, front bedrooms, and sun terrace, you can see lovely uninterrupted views over the Moray Firth. This completely modernized family-run hotel offers high standards of comfort, attentive service, and cuisine prepared from fresh, local, quality produce and seafood.

A typical menu features smoked monkfish salad with melon and strawberries marinated in balsamic and honey, followed by ragout of wild Highland venison in a rosemary-infused red wine sauce on a pureed parsnip with raspberry, and Drambuie parfait with crème anglaise. Ian and Sylvia and their two sons, John and Alexander, are a handsome family. Living up to the B&B's name, the rooms are indeed sunny, and the attention that the Bochels spend on details is impressive.

Each room is individually decorated and spotlessly clean. The color schemes are unusually pleasing to the eye (yellow pillows on blue chairs). Whenever possible, regular visitors are given their favorite rooms—a nice personal touch.

There are always plenty of things to do in the area, from golfing and indulging in a boat trip or two, to some serious beachcombing. (Nairn has earned a reputation for having a mild climate—not exactly Miami Beach, mind you, but warm enough to at least be able to enjoy the sunshine.) In this neck of the woods a favorite pastime is dolphin watching. Numerous historic sites are nearby, including Cawdor Castle, Culloden Battlefield, and Fort George. Of course, Nessie is close by too. And don't forget the Whiskey Trail—several distilleries are nearby, including Glenfarclas, Strathisla, Dallas Dhu, and Speyside Cooperage.

Seabank Bed & Breakfast
Alasdair and Lynn Bruce
6 Bank Street
Plockton
Telephone/Fax: 01599-544221
E-mail: lynn@seabank-plockton.co.uk
Web site: www.Seabank-Plockton.co.uk
Bedrooms: 3, 1 ensuite.
Rates: £20-25 double. **Credit cards:** None. **Open:** Year-round.
Children: Yes. **Pets:** Yes. **Smoking:** No. **Provision for handicapped:** No.
Directions: From Plockton railway station, continue down the hill, past the primary school at the bottom on the right. Seabank is located behind the school. Parking is available behind the house or in the car park.

This small and recently restored cottage boasts a garden that faces directly onto the shore of lovely Loch Carron. Seabank is located in the historic village of Plockton, which is known for both its charm and its spectacular natural surroundings (it was voted Highland Village of the Year in 1994). The popular BBC television series *Hamish MacBeth* was filmed here. (Its star, Robert Carlyle, has since gone onto to even bigger things, including starring roles in *The Full Monty* and, most recently, *Angela's Ashes.*) Plockton is a good base for walking, boat trips, or visiting Skye (the Skye Bridge, now free, is only a short six-mile drive away). Seabank itself is perfectly situated in a quiet part of the village by the water's edge and within easy walking distance of numerous hotels, shops, and restaurants. Most rooms have a view of the loch.

The Shieling
Jane and John MacDonald
Plockton
Telephone/Fax: 01599-544282
E-mail: jane@shieling282.freeserve.co.uk
Web site: www.lochalsh.net/shieling
Bedrooms: 2 rooms, 1 ensuite, 1 private.
Rates: £22.50-25. **Credit cards:** No. **Open:** Easter-late October.
Children: Over age 14. **Pets:** No. **Smoking:** No. **Provision for handicapped:** Suitable for some disabled people; call for arrangements.
Directions: Drive into the village and along the harbor street. Turn right by the village hall, then right again at the end of the road. The Shieling is situated on the edge of the peninsula.

In my humble opinion, the MacDonalds are blessed with one of the finest views in Plockton. Situated on a slight peninsula, the Shieling feels both isolated and safe. The vantage point from the town itself makes it appear very inviting—a tiny, whitewashed cottage on its own (to get here you must follow the footpath along the narrow causeway). In reality, the MacDonalds have a comfortable family home in an exceedingly picturesque historic village, with panoramic views over the loch from their spacious lounge, which in turn leads to the garden. Whichever way you look—toward the village itself or the surrounding loch—the views are mighty impressive. Plockton is an ideal base for touring the surrounding countryside. It's also a gateway to Skye, since the famed island is only a short drive away. But do spend some time in the village of Plockton itself. In recent years it has become a familiar sight to TV watchers in Britain—the popular *Hamish MacBeth* series was shot here. With its palm trees, traditional red telephone booths, and snug cottages, it is a perfect place to relax and do absolutely nothing.

Cloisters
Bob and Audrey Morrison
Church Holme
Talmine
Sutherland
Telephone/Fax: 01847-601286
E-mail: reception@cloistertal.demon.co.uk
Web site: www.cloistertal.demon.co.uk
Bedrooms: 3 rooms, all ensuite.
Rates: £27.50-30 single, £22.50-25 double. **Credit cards:** None. **Open:**
All year. **Children:** From age 12. **Pets:** Yes, if house-trained. **Smoking:**
No. **Provision for handicapped:** 1 room is wheelchair accessible.
Directions: Follow the A9 North sign, then turn off onto the B817 near
Evanton to Bonar Bridge. Take the A836 from Bonar Bridge to Lairg
(approximately 11 miles), and continue on the A836 to Tongue
(approximately 40 miles). Leave Tongue on the A838 causeway, turn
right to Melness and Talmine on unclassified road (about 3 miles).
Pass through Skinnet Pass, with the Craggan Hotel on the left.
Cloisters is ahead on a small road on the left. If you reach Talmine
post office, you have gone too far.

As its name indicates, the Cloisters' former life was that of a nineteenth-century church. Interior archways recall this former life.
Located in the village of Talmine on the Kyle of Tongue, the Cloisters
offers marvelous sea views over inshore islands to Orkney beyond. The
surrounding area is also studded with historic landmarks, from Bronze
Age remains to Clearance villages.

Your hosts have quite a fascinating background. Bob Morrison
was born in Nairn and is a retired architect who spent most of his

working life in Australia's Northern Territory. He plays clarinet with a local jazz group. Audrey is from Aberdeen and is a retired classical ballet teacher who also spent most of her working life in Australia, running her own ballet school in Darwin. Aberdeen-born Iain was raised in Australia and operates Highlander Photographic Safaris, a six day/five night all-inclusive package holiday that offers customized tours tailored to suit various interests, from history and archaeology to wildlife and photography (maximum: 6 passengers).

Continental, vegetarian, or full Scottish breakfast is served either in the dining room or sun lounge overlooking Talmine Bay. Packed lunches can be provided upon request.

The Ceilidh Place
Jean Urquhart
14 West Argyle Street
Ullapool
Telephone: 01854-612103
Fax: 01854-612886
E-mail: stay@theceilidhplace.com
Web site: www.theceilidhplace.co.uk
Bedrooms: 15 rooms in main building.
Rates: £60 pp. **Credit cards:** Yes. **Open:** Year-round. **Children:** Yes. **Pets:** By arrangement. **Smoking:** Yes. **Provision for handicapped:** No.
Directions: Located in the center of the village, just north of the harbor.

It's hard to believe that the Ceilidh Place started out in the 1970s in such a humble way—by serving light refreshments and entertainment in a former boat shed—for today it is one of the premier lodgings in all of Scotland. But more than just a hotel or B&B, the Ceilidh Place is also an excellent restaurant, casual café, pub, art gallery, bookshop, and all-around entertainment center. Light meals and snacks are served cafeteria-style in the café (vegetarian food and local seafood are specialties). The restaurant offers fine dining at its best. There is also an excellent selection of malt whiskies, wines, and ales in the pub. But what really sets the place apart is the ongoing entertainment held throughout the year: concerts, literary events, plays, exhibitions, and slide lectures.

You name it, the Ceilidh Place does it, from traditional Scottish music to the Mississippi Delta blues. The main white two-story building consists of 15 rooms (8 double, 4 twin, and 3 single bedrooms),while the college dormitory-type setting of the clubhouse offers comfort at considerably lower prices—about £15 for a single (breakfast is extra though). It's all very rustic and collegiate in the clubhouse with its bunk beds, wooden furniture, and communal facilities. Ullapool has several sites worth visiting, including the small Ullapool Bookshop and Museum and its larger counterpart, the Ullapool Museum, which has a terrific exhibition on emigration from the Loch Broom area to Nova Scotia.

Summer Isles Hotel
Mark and Gerry Irvine
Achiltibuie
By Ullapool
Telephone: 01854-622282
Fax: 01854-622251
E-mail: info@summerisleshotel.co.uk
Web site: www.summerisleshotel.co.uk
Bedrooms: 13 rooms, all with private bath.
Rates: £75-119. **Credit cards:** MasterCard/Eurocard, VISA. **Open:**
March to mid-October. **Children:** From 8 years. **Pets:** By arrangement.
Smoking: No smoking in dining room. **Provision for handicapped:**
Restricted. **Directions:** From Inverness take the A835 northwest to
Ullapool. Summer Isles is located 10 miles beyond Ullapool. Turn
left onto a single-track road. An additional 15 miles on will bring you
to the village. The hotel is 1 mile past the village entrance on the left.

Summer Isles was originally built during the mid-nineteenth century for the fishing tenants on the Cromarty estate. Since the Irvines
bought it in 1969, it has become a haven of civilization in a stunning
yet remote part of Scotland. The major draws around here are the
Summer Isles' food and the gorgeous scenery. The tiny village of
Achiltibuie consists of a line of white cottages looking over the bay
toward the evocatively named Summer Isles. Although the area is
warmed by the gulf stream, Mark and Gerry are quick to stress that the
weather can change suddenly, from "Arctic to Aegean inside a week,"
so be prepared. The scent of the sea is everywhere. So it's not surpris-
ing to learn that nearly everything on your breakfast and dinner plates
is home-produced or locally caught: scallops, lobsters, crabs, halibut,
turbot, and salmon, as well as venison, brown eggs, and brown bread
fresh from the oven.

The Irvines best sum up the appeal of Summer Isles: "a marvelous amount of nothing to do." Actually there is plenty to do if you enjoy fishing, birdwatching, or walking the trails (anywhere from three to 30 miles). The *Hectoria* is a local cruise boat that takes people around the islands to view seals and rare species of birds. There is also a diving school nearby, or you can take the Irvines' advice and simply relax. Nothing is rushed here. About the only timetable you need to worry about is dinner. It is served promptly at eight o'clock sharp.

ALSO RECOMMENDED

Ballachulish, *Craiglinnhe Guest House.* Lettermore.Telephone: 01855-811270. E-mail: info@craiglinnhe.co.uk. Web site: www.craiglinnhe.co.uk. 5 rooms, all ensuite. Elegant Victorian guesthouse overlooking Loch Linnhe. Excellent food and lodging at reasonable prices.

Ballachulish, *Lyn-Leven Guest House,* John and Priscilla MacLeod, West Laroch, near Fort William. Telephone: 01855-811392. Fax: 01855-811600. E-mail: lynleven@amserve.net. 8 rooms, all ensuite. This modern bungalow with a lovely garden overlooks Loch Leven. Scottish meals are their specialty.

Boat of Garten, *Heathbank—The Victorian House,* Lindsay and Graham Burge. Telephone: 01479-831234. 7 rooms, all ensuite. Turn-of-the-century Victorian country house set in its own gardens. Two of the rooms have fourposter beds and are tastefully decorated with flourishes of period charm. Fresh soups, homemade breads, local game and fish, and Scottish beef and lamb are served to guests.

Culloden Moor, *King of Clubs,* Vanne P. Fraser, Tigh-na-Ceard, Sunnyside, near Inverness. Telephone/Fax: 01463-790476. E-mail: kingofclubs@mail.easynet.co.uk. 2 rooms, both ensuite. Friendly and tastefully decorated, with spacious rooms. Its name derives from their main source of business: custom golf-club makers and repairers. King of Clubs is a 10-minute walk from Culloden battlefield and a 10-minute drive to Inverness town center.

Drumnadrochit, *Drumbuie Farm,* Ian and Caroline Urquhart, Loch Ness. Telephone: 01456-450634. Fax: 01456-450595. E-mail: drumbuie@amserve.net. 3 rooms, all ensuite. Livestock farm; highland cattle. This working farm overlooks Loch Ness.

Fort Augustus, *Fort Augustus Abbey on Loch Ness,* Inverness-shire. Telephone: 01320-366233. Fax: 01320-366228. E-mail: abbey@ monk.co.uk. Web site: www.monk.co.uk. 29 rooms. Simply furnished rooms, Spartan and clean. There is also a game room, television lounge, and "quiet" lounge in addition to a fine restaurant on the premises and a heritage center. Loch Ness cruises can be arranged.

Fort William, *Ashburn House,* Achintore Road. Sandra and Allan

Henderson. Telephone: 01397 706000. Fax: 01397 702024. E-mail: ashburn.house@tinyworld.co.uk. Web site: www.scotland2000.com. 7 rooms, all ensuite. Located a short walk from the High Street, this modernized Victorian house sits on the shore of Loch Linnhe in a quiet part of town and yet it is only a five-minute walk away. Rates range from £30-45 per person.

Kingussie, *The Hermitage Guest House,* David and Marie Taylor, Spey Street. Telephone/Fax: 01540-662137. E-mail: thehermitage@clara.net. The Taylors offer comfortable bedrooms with ensuite facilities, a resident's lounge with log fires on cold evenings, and a large garden with views of the Cairngorm mountains.

Lairg, *Park House,* Margaret and David. Walker, Station Road. Telephone: 01549-402208. Fax: 01549-402693. E-mail: david-walker@park-house.freeserve.co.uk. Web site: www.lairghighlands.org.uk. 3 rooms, all ensuite. Overlooking Loch Shin, the Park House offers spacious rooms and home-cooked meals. Brown trout and salmon fishing or golfing on five local golf courses can be arranged.

Melvaig, *Rua Reidh Lighthouse,* by Gairloch, Ross-shire. Chris Barrett and Fran Cree. Telephone: 01445-771263. E-mail: ruareidh@netcomuk.co.uk. 8 rooms, some ensuite. This is truly getting away from it all. Built in 1910 by a cousin of Robert Louis Stevenson—one of the Lighthouse Stevensons—Rua Reidh is now fully automated and has been converted to provide modern accommodation for the discriminating traveler. It also has a conservatory, 2 sitting rooms with log-burning fires, a kitchen, laundry room, as well as magnificent views over the Minch to Skye and the Western Isles. The entire house can be rented. Note: Rates are based on a room-only basis with breakfast extra at a nominal fee (around £5 each).

Melvich, *Melvich Hotel,* by Thurso. Peter and Annemieke Martin. Telephone: 01641-531206. Fax: 01641-531347. E-mail: melvichtl@aol.com. 14 rooms, all ensuite. Privately owned country hotel, the Melvich Hotel overlooks Melvich Bay looking toward Orkney. The hotel also boasts reportedly the U.K.'s most northerly brew-pub, the Far North Brewery. Among the beers are Split Stone Pale Ale, Fast Reactor, and Edge of Darkness. Day trips to Orkney can be arranged from here.

Plockton, *Plockton Hotel,* Dorothy and Tom Pearson, Harbour Street. Telephone: 01599-544274. Fax: 01599-544475. Web site:

www.host.co.uk. 4 rooms, all ensuite. Small and friendly with lots of atmosphere. 2 of the front bedrooms overlook the loch. The wonderful restaurant offers friendly service, a maritime flavor, and cozy atmosphere. Specialties include local shellfish, especially prawns, and char-grilled steaks.

Rhue, *Suilven Vegetarian Bed & Breakfast,* by Ullapool. Barry Chislett. Telephone: 01854-612955. E-mail: info@bvegb.co.uk. 2 rooms, 1 ensuite. Located 3 miles north of Ullapool in the northwest Highlands, this self-built, architect-designed house incorporates some rather unusual features, such as solar heating. Vegetarian cooked breakfasts are on the menu.

Spean Bridge, *The Braes Guest House,* Tirindrish. Telephone: 01397-712437. 7 rooms, all ensuite. Absolutely lovely guesthouse that offers not only spectacular views of Ben Nevis and comfortable accommodations but also attentive and caring service.

Strathpeffer, *Craigvar,* Margaret S. L. Scott, The Square. Telephone: 01997-421622. Fax: 01997-421796. E-mail: m.s.@gilsmith.demon.co.uk. 3 rooms, all ensuite. Handsome Georgian house overlooking the town square in a former Victorian spa village. Many personal touches, including a fourposter bed.

Strathy Point, *Sharvedda,* P. A. MacAskill, by Thurso. Telephone: 01641-541311. 3 rooms, 2 ensuite. Small working croft with superb views to Orkney and Dunnet Head. Popular with hill walkers and bird-watchers. The large spacious lounge has an open peat fire in the winter. The dinner menu emphasizes traditional locally made foods. Home baking is a specialty.

By **Thurso,** *Aultivullin,* Donald and Margaret MacKay, Strathy Point. Telephone: 01641-541235. 3 rooms. Traditional crofthouse, immaculately and lovingly kept. Among the attractions in the area are a sandy beach at Strathy Bay and grassy dunes.

Ullapool, *Brae Guest House,* Shore Street. Telephone: 01854-612421. 11 rooms, 10 ensuite. Pretty, clean, and cozy. Cruises, sailing, and waterskiing on Loch Broom can be arranged.

Ullapool, *The Sheiling Guest House,* Duncan and Mhairi MacKenzie,

Garve Road. Telephone: 01854-612947. Web site: www.thesheilingul-lapool.co.uk. 6 rooms, all ensuite. Situated above the main road to Ullapool, the Sheiling offers panoramic views of lovely Loch Broom. Cheery bedrooms. The lounge and dining room overlook the loch.

THE HEBRIDES

St. Kilda
inset not to scale

THE HEBRIDES

to St. Kilda
(From Harris
50 miles-80 km)

WESTERN ISLES
(Outer Hebrides)

Butt of Lewis
Port of Ness

Lewis Black House
Shawbost
Barvas
New Tolsta
Carloway
Arnol
Tolsta Head
Dun Carloway Broch
Back
Great Bernera
Breasclete
Uig
Callanish Standing Stones
Stornoway
Brenish
LEWIS
A857
A857
A858
A859
B8011

The Minch

car ferry to Stornoway

SCARP
TARANSAY
Ardvourlie
Sound of Shiant

Luskentyre
Tarbert
SCALPAY
Sound of Taransay
HARRIS
car ferry to Tarbert
PABBAY
Northton
Leverburgh
Rodel
BERNERAY
BORERAY
Newtonferry
Little Minch
Duntulm

N

LOCHMADDY
A865
Lochmaddy
car ferry to Lochmaddy
Quiraing
Staffin
Kilt Rock
Trotternish
RONA
NORTH UIST
Uig
Loch Snizort
Kingsburgh
Sound of Raasay
Balivanich
BENBECULA
Dunvegan Head
Boreraig
Treaslane
Borve
Arnish
Brochel
Dun Caan
Waternish
Edinbane
Skeabost
1,456 ft.
Inner Sound
Dunvegan
Portree
RAASAY
A896
Duirinish
MacLeod's Tables
Inverarish
Howmore
The Braes
SCALPAY
A865
SOUTH UIST
Carbost
Sconser
Kyleakin
A87
Talisker
THE CUILLINS
Broadford
Kylerhea
Daliburgh
Lochboisdale
Minginish
A863
Ludag
car ferry to Lochboisdale
ISLE OF SKYE
SOAY
Elgol
Sleat
Sound of Sleat
Sound of Barra
ERISKAY
A'Chill
Cuillin Sound
Eoligarry
CANNA
Kilmory
Armadale
Ardvasar
Borve
BARRA
Castlebay
RUM
Kinloch
Sound of Canna
Mallaig
VATERSAY
SANDRAY
Sea of the Hebrides
Sound of Rum
A830
Sound of Mingulay
PABBAY
EIGG
Glamisdale
MINGULAY
MUCK
Port Mor
Sound of Eigg
A861

0   15 miles

0   15 kilometers

Skye

Skye. Even the word itself sounds wildly romantic. So much has been written about this famous Hebridean island that sometimes one is at a loss to describe its incandescent beauty, its special aura. For when the light hits a certain way or a rainbow peeks fleetingly from behind swirling clouds, words are not enough.

Traditionally one came to Skye by sea. Nowadays though, contemporary travelers also have the option of driving across the Skye Bridge. While controversial, it is quite an engineering and aesthetic marvel, rising skyward from Kyle of Lochalsh to Kyleakin. For those who insist on catching a ferry to Skye, you can depart the traditional way from either Mallaig, Kylerhea, or the Western Isles.

The capital of Skye is Portree, a handsome town in which there is much to do. There are several fine restaurants, ranging from Indian to vegetarian, as well as numerous craft and gift shops. Probably the most important attraction is the Aros Heritage Centre, which explores the island's tumultuous past. It also contains a fine restaurant and an excellent shop that stocks books and CDs. Gaelic concerts are held here during the summer months. Don't miss the An Tuireann Arts Centre, a combination art gallery and lovely café. Carmina Gadelica on Wentworth Street, Portree's main thoroughfare, is an excellent bookshop, especially strong on titles of local interest.

Skye has many faces. North of Portree, the Trotternish Peninsula offers some of the most spectacular scenery on the island, from the quiet beauty of the Old Man of Storr to the otherworldly rock formations of the Quiraing. Also in the vicinity, Flora MacDonald's grave and monument is located at Kilmuir. (MacDonald was the island heroine who saved Bonnie Prince Charlie's life back in 1745-46.) Duntulm Castle, now a ruin, was once the home of Clan MacDonald. The Museum of Island Life in the crofting township of Staffin is an outdoor living history museum of Skye heritage and customs, while the ferry port of Uig offers daily sailings to the Western Isles.

In western Skye, Dunvegan Castle, home to the chiefs of MacLeod for more than 700 years, has exhibits, gardens, craft shops, a restaurant, and even wildlife cruises. Northwest of Dunvegan, the MacCrimmon Piping Centre at Boreraig commemorates the wonderful gift that the MacCrimmons gave to the world—pibroch, the classical music of the Highland bagpipe. The museum is worth a visit, even for non-music-lovers.

Skye's southern peninsula, Sleat (pronounced "Slate"), is often called "The Garden of Skye," and for good reason. It is a lush area of woodland and greenery. The Clan Donald Visitor Centre houses the Museum of the Isles, which includes a restaurant, shop, and genealogy research library. Down the road from the center is Sabhal Mor Ostaig, Skye's Gaelic college and one of the leading institutions of the modern Gaelic cultural revival. Previously a farm that belonged to the MacDonalds (its name, in fact, translates into "big barn"), Sabhal Mor Ostaig offers short courses in Gaelic music, culture, and heritage.

There's much more to Skye than these few paragraphs suggest. One could spend a lifetime here exploring its corners and still not see everything.

Lime Stone Cottage
Kathie M. McLoughlin
4 Lime Park
Broadford
Telephone/Fax: 01471-822142
E-mail: kathielimepark@btiuternet.com
Bedrooms: 3 rooms, all ensuite.
Rates: £18-25. **Credit cards:** None. **Open:** Year-round. **Children:** Yes.
Pets: No. **Smoking:** Restricted. **Provision for handicapped:** Restricted.
Directions: From the Skye Bridge take the A850 to Broadford. After
passing the Claymore Restaurant, turn left into Lime Park. Turn right
at the Reptile Centre. The cottage is 150 yards on your left.

This small turn-of-the-century crofter's cottage was originally built
for workers at the local lime kiln. You can tell it dates from a different era and mindset—handsome and sturdy in a practical sort of way.
Derelict for many years, it has been lovingly restored to retain its original character while still suiting the needs of modern travelers. It offers
wonderful views over Broadford Bay to Loch Carron and the Scottish
mainland. Kathie offers a comfortable sitting room with log fire for
guests who have learned to appreciate the simple pleasures of life. She
also serves a traditional home-cooked breakfast and caters to visitors
with vegetarian or special diets. Packed lunches are available on
request. Kathie is generous with advice when it comes to suggesting
the many walks and tours offered on the island.

Glenview Inn and Restaurant
Paul and Cathie Booth
Culnacnoc
By Staffin
Telephone: 01470-562248
Fax: 01470-562211
Bedrooms: 5 rooms; 4 ensuite, 1 with private bathroom.
Rates: £20-30. **Credit cards:** VISA, MasterCard, Delta. **Open:** March-November. **Children:** Yes. **Pets:** Yes. **Smoking:** Restricted to residents lounge only. **Provision for handicapped:** No. **Directions:** Off the A855 on the Staffin Road, the Glenview Inn is located 12 miles north of Portree between the Old Man of Storr and the Quiraing.

One of the finest examples of traditional croft architecture, the Glenview Inn was built by a local merchant as a home and village shop. Today the old gentleman still remembers, according to Paul and Cathie Booth, bringing up the supplies landed by steamer from Glasgow in the bay below the inn. Tastefully modernized, this home away from home is located on the northern tip of Skye, in the Trotternish Peninsula. Nearby are two of the island's eeriest rock formations, the Old Man of Storr and the Quiraing. Not surprisingly, walking, climbing, photography, and birdwatching are popular activities here.

For quieter times, you can always enjoy the inn's peaceful sitting room, where you can nurse a local malt in front of the open fire or browse through a wide selection of books and maps. The evening meals are quite impressive, too: how about hot-game haggis with rowanberry jelly and homemade oatcakes or Skye lobster tails sautéed in garlic butter for starters? For entrées consider the braised shank of Scottish lamb cooked Moroccan style with prunes, citrus fruit, and ginger and served on a bed of couscous. The next course could be a warm onion and pepper flan or a baked terrine of wild forest mushrooms with fresh tomatoes, mozzarella, herbs, and sweet potato baked with coconut milk and served with a leaf salad. If you have any room left for dessert, you can always choose between the bread and butter pudding, panna cotta with raspberry sauce, or hot apple and rhubarb pie with custard. For a lighter sendoff, try a plate of Scottish cheeses with biscuits, fruit, and celery. It's all scrumptious.

The Tables Hotel & Restaurant
Dunvegan
Isle of Skye
Telephone/Fax: 01470-521404
E-mail: bookings@tables-hotel.co.uk
Web site: www.gael.net/tableshotel
Bedrooms: 5 rooms, 4 ensuite.
Rates: From £30 pp. **Credit cards:** Yes. **Open:** March-October.
Children: Yes. **Pets:** Yes. **Smoking:** No. **Provision for handicapped:** No.
Directions: One mile from Dunvegan Castle.

Overlooking Loch Dunvegan and the mountain range known as MacLeod's Tables, the Tables houses an award-winning restaurant, a fine selection of good wines and single malts, and a warm peat fire. Vegetarian and vegan dishes are among their specialties. Actually, dining at the Tables—no matter the time of day—always is a joy. A traditional Scottish breakfast may consist of bacon, fried egg, sausage, black pudding, white pudding, potato scone, and tomato, while a vegetarian/vegan breakfast may bring a "sausmix" sausage, fried egg with smoked tofu rashers of bacon, tomatoes, mushroom, potato scone, and baked beans. Other possibilities include porridge, Skye-smoked haddock, Skye kippers, and scrambled tofu with herbs. And that's just the breakfast. For their evening meals, the staff uses local and seasonal produce, and as much Highland and organic meat, poultry, and fish as possible. On Skye, the latter could mean locally caught prawns, scallops, or crab.

Rosedale Hotel
Allison and Paul Rouse
Beaumont Crescent
Portree
Telephone: 01478-613131
Fax: 01478-612531
E-mail: rosedalehotelsky@aol.com
Bedrooms: 19 rooms, all ensuite.
Rates: From £38. **Credit cards:** VISA. **Open:** Early May to mid-October.
Children: Yes. **Pets:** No. **Smoking:** Yes. **Provision for handicapped:** No.
Directions: Located on Portree's harbor front.

Located on the harborfront, the Rosedale is a row of whitewashed fisherman's cottages converted to a small hotel with views directly over the harbor. The staff is efficient and friendly, the rooms snug and warm. The restaurant has received several awards, and features a changing daily menu. The Rosedale has two very comfortable lounges that feature a fine selection of single malts. Of course, the fiery Talisker, Skye's single malt, is available at the bar. The Rosedale boasts a terrific location. Not only do you have the harbor, and indeed, the town of Portree, outside your door, but the rest of the island is also at your disposal. Allison and Paul Rouse hail from Dundee. Paul is a former Scottish rugby player, and Allison was a partner in an Edinburgh law firm for many years. A piece of advice: the interior of the Rosedale is of a labyrinth of hallways and doors, with no seeming order to them. Ask at the front desk if someone can escort you to your room, especially if you're carrying heavy luggage.

Kinloch Lodge
Lord and Lady Macdonald
Sleat
Telephone: 01471-833214
Fax: 01471-833277
E-mail: bookings@kinloch-lodge.co.uk
Web sites: www.kinloch-lodge.co.uk; www.claire-macdonald.com
Bedrooms: 10 rooms, all ensuite, in Kinloch Lodge; 5 rooms, all ensuite, in Kinloch.
Rates: £85-140 pp. for dinner and bed and breakfast in both the Lodge and the New House. **Credit cards:** MasterCard/Eurocard, American Express, VISA, Access. **Open:** Year-round except Christmas. **Children:** Yes. **Pets:** By arrangement. **Smoking:** Not in bedrooms or dining room. **Provision for handicapped:** No. **Directions:** 8 miles south of Broadford on the A851; 10 miles north of Armadale on A851. From the Skye Bridge turn right at the roundabout leading to Portree. Follow the A87 for 5 miles, then turn left onto the A851 to Armadale. The turnoff to Kinloch Lodge is 5 miles down the road on the left. Follow the small road for about a mile. From Armadale Ferry take the A851 to Isle Ornsay and Broadford. Kinloch Lodge is 10 miles north on the righthand side of the road.

Staying at Kinloch Lodge is truly a memorable experience. From the gracious staff to the sumptuous meals, Kinloch represents the finest in Scottish hospitality. Secluded between a wooded hillside and the sea loch on two sides, Kinloch is the ancestral home of Lord Macdonald of Macdonald, High Chief of Clan Donald. He and his writer wife, Claire Macdonald, have run it as a small, personal hotel for nearly 30 years.

This handsome white-painted country house hotel dates back to the early 1600s, when it was built as a farmhouse, which later expanded to a sporting lodge in the nineteenth century. The subtly elegant décor reflects Lady Claire MacDonald's taste—long mirrors, old family portraits on dark green walls, and antiques. Lady Claire, an award-winning journalist and author of more than a dozen best-selling cookbooks, presents a five-course menu each night. Don't be put off by it all, though. Claire is thoroughly down to earth and very funny. She possesses that special gift that allows people to feel instantly at home—no matter how elaborate the circumstances.

Guests help themselves to drinks in the drawing room before dinner, which is served about 8 P.M. The menu changes daily. Typically you have a choice of two first courses (always fish or shellfish), soup, and a choice of two main courses, followed by a choice of two puddings. Cheese, biscuits, and fresh fruit are on the sideboard for guests to help themselves. The daily menu is placed in each bedroom with the wine list; guests are asked to list their room number and their choices by afternoon or early evening.

In 1998 the Macdonalds built a new addition, Kinloch, which is adjacent to the Lodge. Guests staying in Kinloch have breakfast and dinner in the Lodge. Pre-dinner drinks and after-dinner coffee and fudge can be enjoyed in Kinloch's drawing room. In addition to five more rooms, Kinloch also houses the Claire Macdonald Centre for Food and Taste, perfect for those with deep pockets who love to cook. The center offers an annual program of cooking demonstrations, which is limited to about 20 people. Prices range from £300-350 per person and include three nights' dinner, bed and breakfast, and light lunch, with two full mornings of demonstrations.

Hotel Eilean Iarmain (Isle Ornsay Hotel)
Sir Iain and Lady Noble
Isle Ornsay
Sleat
Telephone: 01471-833332
Fax: 01471-833275
Web site: www.eileaniarmain.com
Bedrooms: 16 rooms, including 4 ensuite.
Rates: £90 single, £125 double, £190 ensuite. **Credit cards:** MasterCard, VISA, American Express, Eurocard, Switch. **Open:** Year-round. **Children:** Yes. **Pets:** Well-behaved pets only by private arrangement. **Smoking:** Some bedrooms are nonsmoking. **Provision for handicapped:** Yes. **Directions:** From Mallaig/Armadale ferry turn right onto the A852, then right again at the sign for Isle Ornsay. The hotel is located at the water's edge.

This small whitewashed hotel was built in 1888 and stands on a small bay of Isle Ornsay, on the south peninsula of Skye. It's a tranquil place, with log fires and dinner by candlelight. The rooms are decorated with original features and period furniture. One room has a half-tester canopy bed from nearby Armadale Castle, draped in pretty fabrics. Small touches add considerably to the genial atmosphere, such as complimentary tea, coffee, chocolate, shortbread, hair dryer, toiletries, and robes.

The hotel is owned by Sir Iain Noble, a controversial figure in these parts, who has been a vigorous supporter of Gaelic culture for many years (too aggressive for some islander's tastes, as it turns out). Many of the staff members are Gaelic speakers. All rooms also have on hand samples of Te Bheag whisky. Established by Iain Noble in 1976 to supply the Hebrides, the headquarters of the Gaelic Whiskies (Praban Na Linne) are based at Eilean Iarmain, the only whisky company with its home in Skye. The food at the hotel is fresh. Game and venison come from their own estate, and shellfish are taken straight from the old stone pier just yards from the hotel. Traditional afternoon teas are served every day. The Nobles have recently added several new suites. There is also a small sitting room downstairs. One of the upstairs bedrooms overlooks a view of sea and hills and the lighthouse built by Robert Louis Stevenson's grandfather.

Flodigarry Country House Hotel
Pamela and Andrew Butler
Staffin
Telephone: 01470-552203
Fax: 01470-552301
Web site: www.milford.co.uk/scotland/accom/h-1-1741.html
E-mail: info@flodigarry.co.uk
Bedrooms: 18 rooms, all ensuite. (7 rooms in Flora's Cottage and 11 rooms in the main house.)
Rates: £65-95 double main house, £50-70 Flora MacDonald's Cottage.
Credit cards: VISA, MasterCard, Switch, Delta. **Open:** Year-round.
Children: No. **Pets:** Well-behaved dogs only, but not in public rooms— in the bedrooms and public bar only. **Smoking:** Allowed only in lounges and bar. **Provision for handicapped:** The ground floor bedroom in Flora's Cottage is designed with disabled guests in mind.
Directions: Located off the A855, about 20 miles north of Portree.

This grand old historic house offers great views over Flodigarry Island and across Staffin Bay to the Scottish mainland, accompanied by large doses of good old-fashioned Highland hospitality. Flodigarry is a small crofting village where Gaelic is still spoken. The hotel itself is surrounded by five acres of gardens and mixed woodland. A nineteenth-century mansion, Flodigarry was built as a private house in 1895 by Alexander Livingstone MacDonald on a site adjacent to the cottage where Flora MacDonald had once lived; it has been a hotel since 1928. The old billiard room has been converted into an attractive bar and a conservatory (outdoor terrace) with cast-iron pillars.

The Water Horse Restaurant is cozy and intimate; four-course evening meals and traditional Sunday lunches are served here. The cottage next to the hotel was Flora and her family's home from 1751 to 1759; five of her seven children were born here. The cottage is tastefully renovated and consists of seven ensuite rooms, each uniquely decorated and furnished in period style—wooden olive-green chairs, targe (shield) above the bed, and a fireplace. A ruined broch, at least 500 years old, lies in the hotel garden. Watch out for golden eagles and otters along the seashore. Many fine coastal and hill walks are available from the hotel, including the Quiraing and Trotternish ridge walk. Sea fishing trips can also be arranged.

ALSO RECOMMENDED

Glen Eynort, *The Blue Lobster,* Robert J. Van der Vliet, Glen Eynort. Telephone: 01478-640320. 3 rooms. Charming little cottage by Carbost.

Kilmuir, *Kilmuir House,* Mrs. S. C. Phelps, near Uig. Telephone: 01470-542262. Fax: 01470-542461. E-mail: phelpskilmuirhouseskye@btinternet.com. 3 rooms. Lovely old manse in walled garden overlooking Loch Snizort. Decorated with antiques. Mrs. Phelps uses local produce and her own free-range eggs. Kilmuir is the ideal area for birdwatchers as well as a great place to check out the fabulous sunsets.

Portree, *The Pink Guest House,* 1 Quay Street. Telephone: 01478-612263. Fax: 01478-612181. 9 rooms, 7 ensuite. Lovely accommodation on Portree Harbor.

Sleat, *The Collies,* Patricia Phillips, 4 Camus Cross, Isle Ornsay. Telephone: 01471-833237. 2 rooms. A non-smoking house, The Collies is located in a quiet area overlooking Isle Ornsay Bay. Breakfast includes fresh eggs from the croft and homemade jams.

Talisker, *Talisker House.* Telephone: 01478-640245. Fax: 01478-640214. E-mail: jon_and_ros.wathen@virgin.net. Web site: www.host.co.uk. 4 rooms, all ensuite. Country house on Skye's west coast. Boswell and Johnson visited in 1773. Features spacious rooms and leisurely dinners.

Treaslane, *Auchendinny Guest House,* Ann and Derek Howes, by Portree. Telephone: 01470-532470. Fax: 01470-532470. 7 rooms, all ensuite. Offers wonderful views of the Aird and Trotternish Hills, as well as comfy accommodations. Choice of full, cooked, or continental breakfasts. Vegetarian dishes available on request. Located just off the Portree to Dunvegan Road, beside a tidal loch; hence, the bird life and frolicking seals provide guaranteed free entertainment.

The Western Isles

The Western Isles include Lewis, Harris, North and South Uist, Barra, and Benbecula, a 130-mile long chain of islands northwest of the Scottish mainland. Perhaps it is their very remoteness that has captured the imagination of writers, artists, and travelers for centuries.

Lewis and Harris form one island: Lewis in the north and Harris in the south. The population of Lewis is about 20,000. Harris has only 2,200.

Lewis is largely rolling moorland and gentle hills, along with countless lochs and lochans. The western and eastern coasts tend to be more mountainous, with exposed cliffs hanging over rocky shores. Stornoway, the only real town on the island, contains the premier arts venue in the Western Isles. An Lanntair in the Town Hall along South Beach opened in 1985 and hosts exhibitions, concerts, and theater presentations. It also houses an attractive café.

Some of the most important prehistoric landmarks are located in Lewis. The best known is undoubtedly Callanish, or Calanais, the 5,000 year-old standing stones that are just as impressive as Stonehenge, perhaps more so, for at least up here you can actually get close to the stones.

Harris is an indescribably beautiful island, offering a breathtaking landscape of mountains, lochs, and peatlands. The island is best known for Harris Tweed, even though it is made on both Harris and Lewis. Note: in order for it to be authentic Harris Tweed, it must bear the orb symbol, the mark of the Harris Tweed Association. The lunar landscape and fjord-like lochs of South Harris give way to the gloriously white and clean sandy beaches of Southwest Harris. It is difficult to describe the feeling you get after seeing these usually empty beaches for the first time. They literally take your breath away. A big part of their appeal, of course, is the surprise factor. Who would have thought it possible to see beaches as beautiful as anything in the Mediterranean or other warm-weather climates this far north? Harris is like that, though. It is full of surprises.

Yet each of the islands retains its own particular beauty. Each has something special to offer the visitor who dares to travel this far off the beaten path.

ISLE OF LEWIS

Eshcol Guest House
Neil and Isobel Macarthur
Breasclete
Callanish
Isle of Lewis
Telephone/Fax: 01851-621357
E-mail: neil@eschcol.com
Web site: www.eshcol.com
Bedrooms: 3 rooms, 2 ensuite.
Rates: £33 pp. **Credit cards:** No. **Open:** March-October. **Children:** Over 8. **Pets:** By arrangement. **Smoking:** No. **Provision for handicapped:** All rooms are on ground floor. **Directions:** From Stornoway take the A859 south for 8 miles. At Leurbost turn right and take the A858 an additional 10 miles to Breasclete.

This modern guesthouse is located on a small croft in the small weaving village of Breasclete, on the west coast of Lewis. Quality and service are its calling cards. And since it is situated only two miles from the famous Callanish Standing Stones and three miles from the Carlaway Broch, it is the perfect location for those visitors who wish to explore in-depth the many ancient sites in this area of Lewis, as well as nearby Harris. Your hosts were born and bred in the village of Breasclete and possess considerable knowledge about the area and its history. Neil himself is a native Gaelic speaker. The otherworldly views from the lounge across Loch Roag to Great Bernera are worth the journey alone. The three bedrooms are tastefully decorated. The Macarthurs offer home cooking using produce from their own vegetable garden (in season). It's been said by more than a few visitors that Neil makes the best porridge in Scotland. The Macarthurs would be happy to arrange a local rental car to meet you at the airport or the ferry terminal on request.

Park Guest House
Roddy and Catherine Afrin
30 James Street
Stornoway
Isle of Lewis
Telephone: 01851-702485 or 01851-703482
Fax: 01851-703482
Bedrooms: 9 rooms, 6 ensuite.
Rates: £21-42 single, £21-29 pp double. **Credit cards:** MasterCard/
Eurocard, VISA, Delta. **Open:** Year-round except Christmas Eve to
January 5. **Children:** Yes. **Pets:** No. **Smoking:** Yes. **Provision for handi-
capped:** Yes. **Directions:** Turn left off the the ferry terminal, then left into
Shell Street. Make a right at the first roundabout into James Street. The
guesthouse is 200 yards on the left.

Built in 1883, this handsome stone-built Victorian townhouse offers
some of the finest and most reasonable accommodations in
Stornoway. Both the staff and the management are uniformly friendly
and extremely helpful. The owners, Roddy and Catherine Afrin, come
from interesting backgrounds. Catherine studied at the Glasgow
School of Art, while the youthful and energetic Roddy (usually
dressed in a casual white T-shirt) was a former head chef on an oil rig
in the North Sea. He selects and prepares the locally produced food,
much of it consisting of fresh fish from local fishing boats, as well as
local lamb and venison.
Dinners can consist of dishes such as venison soup, local prawns,
lobster, salmon, and island-grown lamb. Meals are handsomely presented. Look for Stornoway black pudding (blood sausage) at the

breakfast table, along with other hearty fare. The Victorian-era atmosphere is faithfully captured, from the careful restoration of the original woodwork to the attention to detail applied to the bedrooms and public areas. The comfortable sitting room boasts a well-stocked bookshelf.

Within walking distance are the harbor, the library with its extensive local history section, and the Museum nan Eilean, a local history museum that explores the area's rich Gaelic culture and heritage. In addition, the sports center is only yards away, and a full 18-hole golf course is located within the grounds of nearby Lews Castle. The grounds are a lovely place to do a leisurely stroll and admire the trees and rhododendrons planted by Lewis's original owners, Sir James and Lady Matheson.

Ravenswood
Anne MacLeod
12 Matheson Road
Stornoway
Isle of Lewis
Telephone/Fax: 01851-702673
Bedrooms: 3 rooms, 2 ensuite.
Rates: £20-25. **Credit cards:** No. **Open:** Year-round except 2 weeks in October and 2 weeks at Christmas and New Year's. **Children:** Yes. **Pets:** No. **Smoking:** No. **Provision for handicapped:** No. **Directions:** From Stornoway ferry terminal turn left onto the main road to the mini-roundabout. Turn right onto James Street and proceed to a second mini-round. Turn left onto Matheson Road. Ravenswood is on the left-hand side.

This detached Victorian villa, built in 1901, is located on leafy Matheson Road, in a quiet section of Stornoway that is far removed from the commotion of the town center. (I highly recommend that you avoid the busy streets of the town center on weekends when the island's young people descend on Stornoway.) Matheson Road is named after Lady Matheson, whose husband, Sir James Matheson, purchased Lewis in 1844. Mrs. MacLeod, the present owner, tastefully upgraded her home in 1992. It offers a spacious sitting and dining room, attractive and clean rooms, and a relaxing atmosphere. It is also within walking distance of Stornoway's major sites.

ISLE OF HARRIS

Scarista House
Tim and Patricia Martin
Scarista
Isle of Harris
Telephone: 01859-550238
Fax: 01859-550277
E-mail: timandpatricia@scaristahouse.com
Web site: www.scaristahouse.com
Bedrooms: 5 rooms, all ensuite.
Rates: £110-125 single, £75-85 double. **Credit cards:** MasterCard/Eurocard, VISA. **Open:** May-September. **Children:** Yes. **Smoking:** In annex only. **Pets:** Yes by prior arrangement. **Provision for handicapped:** No. **Directions:** 15 minutes southwest of Tarbert on A859.

Scarista House, probably one of the most famous lodgings in all of Scotland, boasts a fascinating history. The original owners, Aberdeen-bred Alison Johnson and her husband, Andrew, converted a derelict old manse, formerly the residence of the local Church of Scotland minister and one of the few landmark buildings in the Western Isles, into a highly acclaimed hotel. Although they sold the hotel in 1989, the often-hilarious story of their hard-earned triumphs and frequent struggles makes for good reading (you can pick up a copy of Alison's *A House By the Shore* at most bookstores throughout Scotland). Today the current owners, Tim and Patricia Martin, have taken up the torch. Their quiet country guesthouse retains its spectacular location overlooking a three-mile shell-sand beach.

All rooms offer excellent views over the garden to the sea beyond. Their library stocks a large collection of books, including many of local interest, for browsing and glows with an open fire. Resident cat Max is particulalry partial to this cozy room. They also make available to their guests record and CD players, but no newspapers, television, or radio (after all, you didn't come all the way to Harris to keep up with the rest of the world, did you?).

Like their predecessors, the Martins serve mainly organic produce, with lots of local fish and shellfish in a menu that changes daily, as well as fresh vegetables and herbs from the walled garden. Your morning eggs are local. Breakfasts usually consist of porridge, yogurt, black pudding, kippers, and fine teas and coffees. All of their breads, cakes, and jam are homemade, as are their marmalade, ice cream, and yogurt. There is a solid wine list too, consisting of about 50 selections. All in all, Scarista is a special kind of place. Self-catering can also be arranged.

ALSO RECOMMENDED

Castlebay, *Tigh-na-Mara,* Linda and Archie Maclean, Isle of Barra. Telephone: 01871-810304. 5 rooms, all ensuite. Comfortable old stone building offering both breakfast and evening meals.

Lochmaddy, *The Old Courthouse,* Margaret Johnson, North Uist. Telephone: 01876-500358. 4 rooms, all ensuite. In an earlier life this colorful B&B functioned as both courthouse and jail for all of the Western Isles. Gaelic is spoken here. Mrs. Johnson has earned a reputation as an excellent cook, Particularly noteworthy are her vegetarian meals. The visitor center, Taigh Chearsahagh, located near the pier, is a combination local history museum, art gallery, shop, and café.

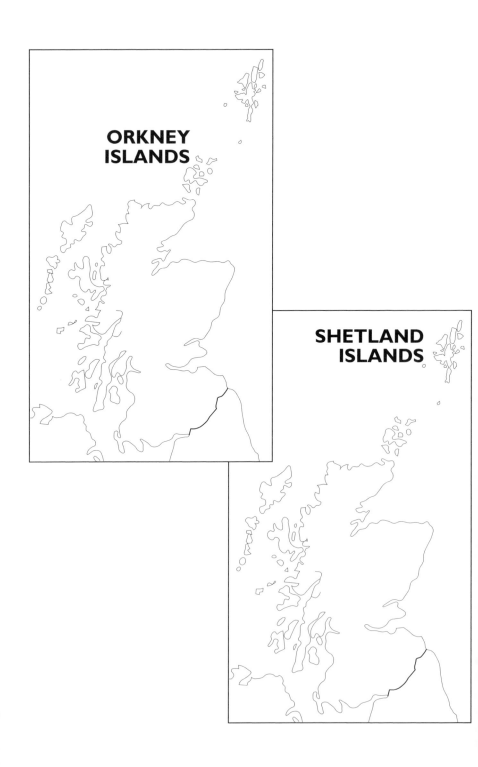

ORKNEY ISLANDS

SHETLAND ISLANDS

Orkney & Shetland

North of the Scottish mainland lies a chain of islands that appears more Scandinavian than Scottish. The lilt of their singsong accent reminds one of Norway. The place-names are largely Scandinavian, as are the island folklore and legends, and even the fiddling tradition smacks of Scandinavian rhythms and scales.

Other images linger in the mind's eye: long summer nights, prehistoric standing stones, the warm glow emanating from St. Magnus' Cathedral, and a Viking boat in Lerwick harbor.

Orkney consists of about 70 islands, most of them green, fertile, and flat. Kirkwall, the capital, is home to the prestigious St. Magnus Festival, a major arts fest held each June and one of the finest in Britain. Many of the concerts and musical events take place in the breathtakingly beautiful St. Magnus Cathedral. Stromness is irresistibly gorgeous, a picture-postcard town of neat stone houses on narrow winding lanes that tumble down to the sea, sort of an Orcadian version of Dylan Thomas's fictitious Welsh village of Llareggub. One sometimes forgets that places like this really do exist.

Beyond the towns themselves are numerous prehistoric sites scattered throughout the islands: the Stone Age village of Skara Brae, the Neolithic burial chamber of Maes Howe, the Standing Stones of Stenness, and the Ring of Brodgar. All remind us just how long these far-away islands have been populated.

About 60 miles north of Orkney is Shetland. These 100 or so islands are considerably rougher and wilder, and more mountainous, than their gentler neighbor to the south.

Lerwick is the commercial capital of Shetland, a small big town of about 7,500 people that is still enjoying the prosperity that has arrived with the North Sea oil boom. The Shetland Room in the Shetland Library and Museum harbors a vast collection of local literature.

Around Shetland don't miss the magnificent Mousa Broch, an impressive fortress that stood guard on the tiny island of Mousa for

2,000 years. It is considered the best-preserved fortress in Scotland. Meanwhile, at the southern tip of mainland Shetland, at Sumburgh Head, is another equally impressive historic monument. Jarlshof was continuously occupied for more than 4,000 years; the buildings range from Norse long house to medieval farmstead.

Busta House Hotel
Joseph Rocks
Busta
Brae
Shetland
Telephone: 01806-522506
Fax: 01806-522588
E-mail: reservations@bustahouse.com
Web site: www.bustahouse.com
Bedrooms: 22, all ensuite.
Rates: From £75-100 single (per room), £110-160 double (per room).
Credit cards: All major credit cards. **Open:** Year-round except Christmas and New Year's. **Children:** Yes. **Pets:** Yes. **Smoking:** Yes. **Provision for handicapped:** No. **Directions:** 22 miles north of Sumburgh Airport on the A970, about one-half mile outside of Brae.

This historic building with great views is set in a sixteenth-century laird's house complete with walled gardens and private piers. The Long Room, or main lounge, serves pre-dinner drinks, coffee, and single malts. The library on the first floor is a non-smoking lounge while the studio on the second floor is not only a meeting room but also home to Busta House Photography, run by Veronica Rocks. Busta House is especially known for Pitcairn Restaurant's four-course dinner menu (around £30 per person). The menu, which changes daily, includes homemade yellow split-pea soup, followed by an organic smoked Shetland salmon with brown bread. Entrees range from char-grilled Orkney Gold filet steak with garlic and pink peppercorn butter and Stilton cheese to Shetland king scallops. Don't forget to leave room for dessert, such as the apricot bread and butter pudding.

Lav'rockha Guest House
John D. Webster
Inganess Road
St. Ola
Kirkwall
Orkney
Telephone/Fax: 01856-876103
E-mail: lavrockha@orkney.com
Web site: www.lavrockha.co.uk
Bedrooms: 5 rooms, all ensuite.
Rates: £32-35 single, £23-26 double. **Credit cards:** VISA, MasterCard.
Open: Year-round. **Children:** Well-behaved children only. There is a £6 charge for children ages two to twelve years, sharing with adults; children under age two stay free. **Pets:** Guide dogs only. **Smoking:** No. **Provision for handicapped:** Unassisted wheelchair access. Wheelchair-friendly entrance and ground floor. **Directions:** Five minutes from Kirkwall Airport. On entering town, Inganess Road is the first road on the right. The guesthouse is located about 100 meters on the right.

Convenient to the airport, ferries to the northern isles, and other forms of transport, Lav'rockha offers comfortable accommodations at affordable rates. It's less than a mile from the town center and a short walk from Highland Park Distillery & Visitor Centre, the northernmost distillery in Scotland. Mr. Webster runs a simple and clean home, with no pretensions. The private resident's lounge has both television and video player, while business guests have access to both fax and e-mail services. In addition, the enclosed outdoor play area is ideal for children.

Stromabank Hotel
Maureen White
Longhope
Hoy
Telephone: 01856-701494
E-mail: enquiries@stromabank.fsnet.co.uk
Web site: www.stromabank.co.uk
Bedrooms: 4 rooms, all ensuite.
Rates: £27 double. **Credit cards:** VISA, MasterCard, Delta. **Open:** Year-round. **Children:** Yes (reduced rates available). **Pets:** Yes. **Smoking:** In the lounge area. **Provision for handicapped:** Partially. **Directions:** Driving from Moaness or Lyness piers in Hoy, take route B9047 toward Longhope. Continue straight uphill in Longhope. The hotel is on your left.

This small, family-run hotel serves homemade meals and hosts regular music evenings with local musicians. Since Orkney has a great musical tradition, this is a real bonus. The island of Hoy itself is truly a nature lover's paradise. The hotel is located near a 9,000-acre nature preserve and various archeological remains as well as wildlife. The most dramatic site is probably the Old Man of Hoy, a rock stack that stands some 450 feet high. Nearby is St. John's Head, the highest vertical cliff face in Britain. Also nearby is Rackwick Bay, considered by many (including classical composer Peter Maxwell Davies, who wrote a piece about it and for many years lived on Hoy) the most beautiful place in Orkney.

Stoneyquoy Farm B&B
Louise and Arthur Budge
Lyness
Isle of Hoy
Orkney
Telephone/Fax: 01856-791234
E-mail: visithoy@hotmail.com
Web site: www.visithoy.com
Bedrooms: 4 rooms, all ensuite or with shared facilities.
Rates: £20 pp. **Credit cards:** None. **Open:** All year. **Children:** Yes. **Pets:**
No. **Smoking:** No. **Provision for handicapped:** No. **Directions:** From
Orkney's Houton pier take the ferry to Lyness on the island of Hoy.
Drive 3 miles towards Longhope. The farm is on the right side.

This nicely appointed farmhouse and 200-acre beef farm offers an
interesting mix of Orcadian and Dutch hospitality. Arthur, a native
Orcadian, took over the farm from his parents in 1974. Louise is Dutch
and came to Scotland as a tourist about 25 years ago and has been here
ever since. A member of the Orkney Tourist Guides Association, she
offers personally guided tours of Hoy and the islands, and can answer
most any question put to her about Orkney. The house is furnished
with antiques, Orkney chairs (a distinctive type of high-backed chair
manufactured in Orkney), an open fire in the sitting room, and many
reading materials, as well as board games, a music center, and television. Louise and Arthur often invite guests to join them on evening
walks to view their cattle. For evening meals Louise prefers to use
Orkney produce whenever possible (soup is her specialty), and serves
Dutch coffee after dinner. Hoy is Orkney's largest outer island (about
26 miles long by 5 miles wide), with a population of only 450.

ALSO RECOMMENDED

Lerwick, *Glen Orchy Guest House,* Joan and Trevor Howarth, 20 Knab Road, Shetland. Telephone/Fax: 01595-692031. E-mail: glenorchy.house @virgin.net. Web site: www.guesthouselerwick.com. 24 rooms, all ensuite. This quiet B&B on the south side of Lerwick is located near the town center and a short distance from a nine-hole golf course.

Lerwick, *Knysa Guest House,* 6 Burgh Road. Telephone: 01595-694865. 4 rooms. Offering friendly service and hearty breakfasts, this substantially built home is located in a quiet residential section of town, a short walk from the town center.

Orphir, *Chinegar,* Mr. and Mrs. Wallington, Orkney. Telephone: 01856-811236. 1 room. Working croft located midway between Kirkwall and Stromness, overlooking Scapa Flow. Includes an artist's studio and the warm glow of a peat fire. Nearby is the Round Kirk, Scotland's only circular medieval church, which stands next to Earl's Bu, a Viking drinking hall. You can learn more about the Norse roots of Orkney and its wonderful collection of Viking tales at the Orkneyinga Saga Experience, a new interpretation center.

St. Margaret's Hope, *Creel Restaurant & Rooms,* Joyce and Alan Craigie, Front Road, South Ronaldsay, Orkney. Telephone: 01856-831311. 3 rooms, all ensuite. E-mail: alan@thecreel.freeserve.co.uk. Website: www.orknet.co.uk. This small family-run and highly acclaimed seafront restaurant, whitewashed and gabled, provides truly innovative modern cooking, although traditional Orcadian influences, such as Orcadian crab soup, are not overlooked either. The excellent menu changes daily according to availability. Two of the spacious rooms offer sea views.

Stenness, *The Mill of Eyrland,* Orkney. Telephone: 01856-850136. Fax: 01856-851633. E-mail: kenandmorag@millofeyrland.demon.co.uk. Web site: www.orknet.co.uk/mill. 3 rooms, 2 ensuite. Converted mill set amid lovely gardens located only three miles from Stromness. Built in 1861, the mill served the Stenness and Orphir communities for more than a century. Stay here and you'll know that it's no typical B&B.

Index

TRAVEL NOTES

TRAVEL NOTES

TRAVEL NOTES

TRAVEL NOTES

TRAVEL NOTES

TRAVEL NOTES